Stained Glass Sourcebook

QUARRY

First published in the United States of America by
Quarry Books, an imprint of
Rockport Publishers, Inc.
33 Commercial Street
Gloucester, Massachusetts 01930-5089
Telephone: (978) 282-9590
Fax: (978) 283-2742
www.rockpub.com

Library of Congress Cataloging-in-Publication data available

ISBN 1-59253-034-6

10 9 8 7 6 5 4 3 2

Cover Design: Wilson Harvey, London [+44 (0)20 7420 7700]
Cover Photography: Bobbie Bush Photography, www.bobbiebush.com

Grateful acknowledgment is given to Giorgetta McRee and Livia McRee for their work from *Stained Glass: Exploring New Techniques and New Materials* on pages 6-107 and 284-298; to Chris Peterson for his work from *The Art of Stained Glass: Designs from 21 Top Glass Artists* on pages 108-241; and to Stephen Knapp for his work from *The Art of Glass: Integrating Architecture and Glass* on pages 244-283.

Printed in China

Stained Glass Sourcebook

GLOUCESTER MASSACHUSETTS

QUARRY BOOKS

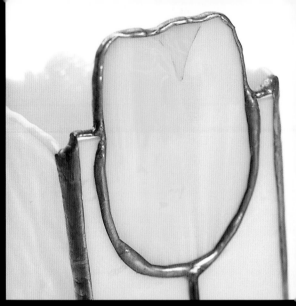

Contents

exploring GLASS

Glass art has a timeless appeal; the mention of stained glass brings to mind antique cathedral windows and Tiffany lampshades. If glass calls to you, don't be intimidated by the seeming complexity of the craft. You'll need relatively few tools to begin, and once you've learned a few simple techniques, you'll be well on your way to discovering the rewards of this art form.

Glass work can be divided into three categories: *cold glass*, *warm glass*, and *hot glass*. In this book, we'll explore cold and warm glass techniques. Cold glass refers to working with glass at room temperature; this includes traditional soldered stained glass and surface decorating techniques such as painting and etching. Warm glass refers to fusing, slumping, and other kiln techniques; glass is heated just enough to soften and gently form it. Hot glass techniques involve a furnace, which can reach temperatures above 2000°F (1100°C); glassblowing falls into this category. Sometimes within the art glass community, "warm" and "hot" aren't differentiated, but are simply referred to as hot glass.

The projects in the cold glass section are intended to explore the many possibilities for expanding upon traditional techniques and styles. The projects in the warm glass section are intended to

introduce kiln work to the beginner. The basic techniques sections are intended to be handy reference manuals to be used again and again—each technique is described step by step, so that if you encounter a problem while you work, you can skip to the part you need with ease.

Finally, the gallery at the end of the book features gorgeous contemporary work from glass artists around the world. We hope that it inspires you to experiment, create, and learn more about glass art.

COLD GLASS
BASIC TECHNIQUES

WHAT IS STAINED GLASS?

Glass is a simple, natural material. It is created when silica—sand—is melted. By mixing minerals with silica, colored or "stained" glass is made. Iron yields green glass; selenium or gold yields red; soda and lime are used to make clear glass. Once molten, the glass mixture is then rolled into a sheet by hand or machine. Using this simple procedure, artisans around the world have created glass for centuries. These days, glass is available in a dazzling variety of colors, textures, and finishes, and the best part of it is that each piece is unique.

GETTING STARTED

SETTING UP A WORK SPACE

Not every artist can have a spacious studio filled with the latest gadgets. Not to worry—there are only a few things that are crucial to stained glass work:

- An electrical outlet will be necessary for plugging in a soldering iron.
- Good lighting from several sources, such as an overhead fixture and a smaller, adjustable lamp, is extremely helpful.
- Excellent ventilation is vital—preferably from a fan installed in a window—to funnel soldering fumes away from the work area. Also, when soldering, set up an additional table fan to blow across the work-table toward the window.
- A flat, level work surface will ensure that leaded lines are even, because molten lead follows gravity.

BASIC STAINED GLASS TOOLS AND SUPPLIES

As with any well-established art, there are many specialty tools available for working with stained glass. However, there are only a few simple tools that are essential:

01. *Safety goggles* are crucial for eye protection when working with glass. Shards can fly up unexpectedly. (Not shown.)
02. *Rubber gloves* protect hands from chemicals, such as flux or patina. Heavier gloves with a rubberized gripping aid should be used when handling glass. (Not shown.)
03. *Homosote board* is made out of paper. It's available at hardware stores and building centers and comes in large sheets $1/2$" (1 cm) thick. It is commonly used in schools as bulletin boards because it holds up well when used with push pins. To prepare a homosote work surface, cut it to an appropriate size for your table. Then, make a 90-degree brace by nailing two pieces of narrow, $1/4$" (6 mm) thick wood in one of the corners. This properly squared space is helpful to hold pieces of a project tightly together.
04. *Pushpins* are very useful for holding individual pieces of foiled glass tightly together during assembly. They are also used on homosote board.
05. *Glass cutters* range from the simple ball-ended wheel cutter seen opposite to more sophisticated circle and straightedge cutters. Though they're called cutters, they actually just score glass. Tungsten-carbide wheels are best, as they produce an excellent score that requires less pressure than less expensive steel or carbide wheels. Having to press too hard for a good score will inevitably lead to a bad break.
06. *Breakers* are used to snap glass along any scored lines.
07. *Running pliers* are especially helpful when breaking along straight scored lines.
08. *Groziers* are serrated pliers that are used to grind away or "groze" the edges of cut glass to perfect the shape.

09. *Medium-grade sandpaper* for metal can be used to refine the edges of glass pieces before foiling them. Grinders are electrical machines with diamond heads that make the job easier, but aren't necessary. Other items can be used, too, such as metal files, sharpening stones, or a Dremel MiniMite fitted with a fine grinding tip. Experiment to see which tools work best for you. (not shown)

10. Use a *bench brush* to sweep away glass shards from the work surface on a regular basis. (not shown)

11. *Copper foil* is an adhesive tape that is used to wrap the edges of pieces of glass that need to be soldered.

12. Use a *burnisher* to press foil into place; the back of a spoon will do in a pinch.

13. *Flux and brushes* for applying it are needed to prepare the surface of copper foil before soldering. The foil is coated with a non metallic oxide film that often impedes solder from properly binding with the copper, causing it to flow unevenly when melted; applying flux prevents uneven solder flow.

14. A *soldering iron* is used to melt solder along foiled seams. Iron tips come in various sizes, and the type used depends on personal preference. Smaller $1/4$" (6 mm) tips are better for reaching smaller places and make it easier to control the flow of lead.

15. *Solder* is composed of tin and lead and is used to attach pieces of foiled glass together.

16. *Tinning blocks* are made of ammonium chloride and are used to clean and "tin" soldering iron tips. Iron tips become corroded with use, so it is necessary to wipe them off on a tinning block; this causes a chemical reaction that cleans and coats the iron tip with a thin protective coat of solder. One will last for life.

17. *Patinas* are available in many colors, such as black or verdigris, and they are used to color the soldered areas of finished works.

18. *Polish* for metal is used to protect, clean, and brighten soldered seams We highly recommend Simichrome, which is available from stained glass suppliers.

19. *Glass*, of course! Shown above are just a few of the patterns, finishes, and textures available.

THE COPPER-FOIL METHOD

Traditionally, stained glass was assembled using strips of lead called *lead came*—an awkward technique that precluded the possibility of intricate, delicate designs because of the lead came's bulk and lack of pliability. This is why many old stained glass windows have intricately painted details on large pieces of glass. In addition, only the joints can be soldered in a lead came piece. Ultrathin, flexible copper foil enables stained glass artists to create beautifully intricate pieces that are structurally sound because all the seams are completely soldered.

SAFETY! SAFETY! SAFETY!

Stained glass work involves sharp edges, chemicals, and fumes. Develop good work habits from the beginning to ensure a safe and healthy environment. Here are some basic guidelines for working with glass:

- Store glass wrapped in paper to cover sharp edges.
- Store tools and chemicals out of the reach of children and animals.
- Vacuum the work area regularly so that shards don't find their way into the rest of the house.
- Wear work gloves when handling glass as much as possible.
- Always wear safety goggles when cutting or breaking glass.
- Always use a bench brush to wipe away glass bits while cutting—never use your hands. Minor cuts will add up quickly when working with glass!
- Always wash up after handling lead and chemicals, and never eat in the work area.
- Soldering creates fumes that contain lead—without proper ventilation, these fumes can be extremely toxic. **Proper ventilation is the most important safety precaution.**

PREPARING PATTERNS

The first step in creating a stained glass work is to select a pattern. There are numerous books available with many beautiful patterns from which to choose (see Resources on page 299). There is also a pattern section in this book, starting on page 284.

Stained glass patterns need to be duplicated for each project. One will be cut apart and used as a template to create scoring guidelines on the glass. The other will be kept intact and used as reference while cutting and assembling the piece. It's also helpful to plan the color scheme of the project on a third copy, using crayons or markers.

SELECTING GLASS

The sheer variety of colors and textures of glass available today can be both exhilarating and daunting. Glass can be streaked, textured with bumps or ripples, embossed with patterns such as leaves, embedded with bubbles or crackles, or have an opalescent surface sheen. Don't be overwhelmed by all these choices—just keep a few things in mind when selecting glass:

1. When selecting glass for a particular pattern, think about where the finished piece will be displayed. What other colors will surround it? Will the light source be natural or artificial? Try to examine the glass in an area of the store that most closely approximates the display conditions.

2. If it will be displayed in a window, hold the glass up to the light to check translucency. Is the color rich enough? Glass looks completely different when stacked up in a store. That seemingly boring, solid color may glow beautifully and reveal hidden streaks when held up to the light.

3. If the finished piece will be displayed against a wall, try using opaque or opalescent glass, which retain their beauty when they're not backlit.

4. If the project is a lamp, which will be seen when lit and unlit, try to find glass that looks good both ways.

Break a straight cut using running pliers. Notice how the center mark on the pliers is aligned with the scored line.

To cut glass along a curve, remove the excess in several gently sloping pieces.

SCORING AND BREAKING ALONG A STRAIGHT LINE

Scoring and breaking glass is perhaps the most intimidating part of the process for a new stained glass artist. It requires patience, practice, and most importantly, confidence. Get a feel for the technique by practicing on scrap glass or inexpensive picture frame glass.

1. Use a straightedge, such as a metal ruler, rather than a marked line as a guide. This will ensure the cut is perfectly straight.

2. Next, put on safety goggles. Then, hold the glass cutter vertically between your index and third finger, as shown here. Position the cutter at the edge farthest from you, next to the ruler. Press down firmly on the glass, but not too firmly—about 10 pounds of pressure. Try pressing down on a scale to get a feel for this amount of pressure.

3. Continue holding the cutter vertically and slowly draw it toward you. Try to apply firm, even pressure all the while. Too much pressure will result in a grating sound and chips along the scored line. The proper amount of pressure will result in a singing sound, and the scored line will look like a light scratch mark. Too little pressure, and the scored line may be hardly visible. Never go over a score line more than once. This will damage the cutter wheel and result in a bad break. Any imperfections in the cut line can be grozed off later.

4. Use the ball end of the cutter to lightly tap along the scored line.

5. To break a straight cut, use running pliers. Hold the glass steady with one hand, and align the center mark on the pliers over the scored line at the bottom edge of the glass sheet with the other hand. Then, gently squeeze the handle of the pliers.

SCORING AND BREAKING AROUND A PATTERN

1. First the glass needs to be marked. Place the template under the glass if it is fairly translucent, or use double-sided tape to adhere it to the surface if the glass is opaque or very dark. Then use a fine-tipped permanent marker to trace the template outline on the glass. Don't worry—the marks will come off when washed. Water-soluble markers tend to smear on glass. Be sure to center the pattern marking on a piece of glass that isn't too much larger than needed.

2. Put on safety goggles. Beginning at the top edge of the pattern marking, score along the edge of the pattern and off the glass once you come close to an edge, or before cutting around too much of the pattern. The excess glass will need to be removed in pieces.

3. Continue cutting around the pattern and off the edge of the glass until the whole piece is scored.

4. Using the ball end of the cutter, tap along the scored lines.

5. Working around the pattern, use a breaker to remove the excess glass. The breaker should be held perpendicular to the scored line, and placed at the end of the score line nearest you. Hold the glass steady with one hand, and hold the breaker firmly with the other; do not squeeze. Then, using both hands, separate the glass with a smooth downward motion. In the beginning, it may be more effective to break the pieces off by hand, because it is easier to feel resistant areas; tap along that area to deepen the score, and try to separate the glass again.

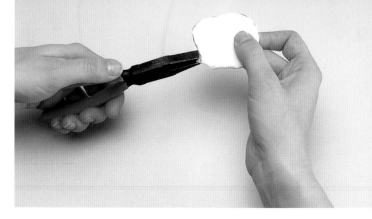

Gently chew away the excess glass using the pattern marking as a guideline.

SCORING AND BREAKING TIPS

Not every pattern is made of straight edges and gentle curves. Patterns that have fine points, circles, or semicircles take more time and patience to cut successfully. Don't be discouraged if glass breaks where it's not supposed to when cutting more complex pattern pieces—sometimes glass has inherent stress lines or fractures. In these cases, try to use the glass in a different way than planned.

Get to know glass, and in time you will be able to tell with ease what it can and can't do—and you'll even learn to predict those stress points!

• *Scoring points*: Points are a delicate area and generally won't withstand the pressure of a breaker. Always break the glass at the edge farthest from the point.
• *Scoring curves*: Inside curves in a pattern will need to be broken away in pieces to avoid a bad break. Score the glass according to the pattern as normal, but also score concentric curved lines within the inside curve, approximately ⅛" (3 mm) apart. Then, use the breaker to carefully nip the excess glass away in these ⅛" (3 mm) increments.

GROZING GLASS FOR A PERFECT FIT

Groziers are pliers with serrated jaws designed to gently chew and chip away at the edges of a cut piece of glass. The edges of cut glass shapes need to be refined to precisely fit within the project template. Therefore, grozing is a crucial step in creating a structurally sound piece of work in which all the pieces fit together perfectly.

1. Put on safety goggles. Arrange all the cut project pieces on the template.

2. Begin with one of the outer pieces. Use the tip of the grozier to remove any bumps along the edge of the glass that protrude past the template outline.

3. After the larger bumps have been removed, continue grozing until the piece matches the template as closely as possible. Don't apply too much pressure, and don't try to remove too much at once. This will cause the glass to chip.

4. Use a piece of medium-grade sandpaper suitable for metal surfaces or an electrical grinder to smooth the edges of the pieces further, so that they fit together like a puzzle.

5. Because foil is soft and easily torn, a smooth edge aids adhesion. When making three-dimensional forms such as boxes, hold adjoining sides together to make sure the edges abut perfectly. Don't overlap the edges—the outside seam should create a groove, which will eventually be filled with solder.

FOILING GLASS

Copper foil is a paper-backed, adhesive metal tape available in several sizes, from ³/₁₆" (4.5 mm) to ½" (1 cm). It can have straight or decorative scalloped edges. Though all foils are copper, some are coated with brass or silver. Color choice depends on personal preference; you'll discover which you like best.

Foils also have either a silver or black backing. Because the backing color is visible after soldering in glass pieces that are translucent, silver-backed foil is good for lighter colors of glass and mirror. Blackbacked foils are good for darker glass because the color minimizes the visibility of the foil.

Make sure foiled edges are smooth and flat against the glass.

Notice where the pieces are tacked and how the foiled seams are still visible under the thin tinned layer.

Try using silver and black foil on the same type of glass; when viewed together, the glass with the blackbacked foiling will appear to be darker than the silver-backed one. This is an easy way to add depth and shaded details to a piece.

Also keep in mind that the width of a soldered seam depends on the size of the foil used; the wider the foil, the wider the seam. Try using different kinds of foils within the same project.

Before foiling glass, make sure the pieces are clean, dry, and free of oils or glass particles.

1. Begin foiling a glass piece about ¹/₄" (6 mm) from the end of one edge. Never begin at corners because foiled seams in these high-stress areas are likely to peel up. Center the foil on the edge of the glass and apply it slowly, pressing it to the edge and removing the paper backing as you move along.

2. Gently ease the foil around the corner, so as not to tear it. Then, crimp the foil down over the sides of the glass piece, using your fingers, from the starting point to the first corner.

3. Then, continue foiling the second edge of the glass, easing the foil around the next corner; then go back and crimp the second edge. Continue until the piece is completely foiled. Overlap the end of the foil ¹/₄" (6 mm) over the starting point.

4. Use a burnisher to press all the foiled areas along the edges and sides of the glass firmly in place.

TACKING AND TINNING

Once the glass pieces of a project are foiled, they are ready to be tacked together. This prevents the pieces from shifting during the next phase of the process, which is called *tinning*.

Tinning involves melting a thin layer of solder along all foiled areas. This strengthens the bonds between the glass pieces because the solder seeps into the crevice between pieces. Tinning also creates a base coat for beading, which results in smoother soldered lines.

1. Begin by arranging the pieces on homosote board, and use pushpins to keep them snugly together.

2. Apply flux to the foiled seams at the points where the glass pieces meet.

3. Unwind some solder from the roll, and melt off a small amount using the tip of the iron. The solder should adhere to the iron; if it doesn't, the iron isn't hot enough.

4. Touch the fluxed areas with the tip of the iron, allowing the solder to flow over the area. This serves to tack the piece together.

5. Flux all the foiled seams.

6. Melt off small amounts of solder as needed, and run the tip of the iron along the foiled seams; use just enough solder to coat them. Remember to do the back and underside of the piece.

MAKING BOXES AND THREE-DIMENSIONAL FORMS

To make boxes or other pieces with 90-degree angles, it helps to construct a right-angle holder like the one seen below, which holds the piece steady so that you have both hands free to work. It also ensures that the piece is squared during the tacking and tinning process when the seams are still flexible.

1. Always solder the seam that is parallel to the work surface because the solder will run toward it when melted.

2. Bead the interior seams of a box shape before tacking the fourth side in place. It will be much easier to maneuver inside, leaving only the last side to bead once the box is assembled.

3. To make a box or form that doesn't have 90-degree angles, use a nonmetal container stuffed with paper towels instead of a right-angle holder to hold it steady while you work. Tack two sides together, and then set them in the cradle of twisted and bunched paper towels. Use the paper towels to brace the piece at the bottom only, making sure that it is level.

When making square shapes, the foiled edges of the glass pieces abut each other to form a right angle, rather than overlapping. The crevices are then filled with solder and built up to form the seam.

BEADING

The final step in soldering a stained glass piece is to create the beads—the rounded seams between the glass pieces. The traditional method of beading is best for small, intricate areas because there's less chance of overheating the solder. The trouble with using this method for larger beads is that the solder often becomes overheated. This causes it to seep between the seams of the foiled pieces because it won't hold its shape. The solder then needs to cool off and solidify before it can be gathered up with the iron tip. Solder behaves like mercury when liquefied and runs away in small beads and drips. Giorgetta McRee developed a new technique for making straight or long beads. It's an easier method that results in smoother beads because the solder is less likely to overheat, and therefore, it doesn't need to be worked as much.

Traditional beading method for small intricate beads:
1. Touch the tip of the iron across the parallel, tinned seam.
2. At the same time, position a strip of solder next to the tip of the iron.
3. Move the iron slowly along the seam, allowing the solder to melt evenly along the foil.

McRee beading method for straight or long beads:
1. Apply flux to the tinned seam.
2. Unwind a strip of solder the length of the seam, and use the iron to "cut" it off.
3. Tack the strip in place along the seam by melting the solder strip slightly.
4. Create the bead by running the tip of the iron along the solder strip to melt it.

To begin, this strip of solder is just barely tacked in place. Run the tip of the iron along the edges to set it, and then let it cool before continuing to smooth it out.

FINISHING TOUCHES

As with all artistic endeavors, it's often the finishing touches that pull a design together or set a piece apart from the rest. With stained glass, you'll want to treat the soldered seams because they will begin to oxidize if left alone. This oxidation results in uneven, splotchy dark spots on the silver solder. You may also want to consider framing your work, especially if it is a decorative panel that you'd like to hang rather than install. Other finishing options include:

Patina: There are several kinds of patina available. Solder can be antiqued, colored black, copper, verdigris, brass, gray, or simply polished to retain the silver color. To apply patina, first pour it in a glass bowl and heat it on a medium setting in a microwave for ten to thirty seconds or until warm. Be careful not to overheat it. Heat facilitates the antiquing process, so additional applications won't be necessary to deepen the color. If you're working quickly and the beaded areas are still warm, heating the patina isn't necessary. Then, use a cotton swab or flux brush to slowly add patina to the seams. Build up the finish as desired. Wipe off any excess that might have seeped onto the glass; it can create a haze that's difficult to remove. Let it sit at least thirty minutes, and then rinse the piece with water.

Polishing: Use Simichrome polish to brighten and protect a patina finish. Apply several small dabs to a section of solder using a cotton swab, and then gently rub it in. Don't polish too hard or too long because the patina may start to come off.

IRON TIPS AND TEMPERATURES

Soldering irons are available in 80-watt or 100-watt voltage capability. It's best to purchase a separate temperature regulator, which can be used with any iron, rather than buying one that has a built-in regulator. These have a tendency to burn out before the iron does. Temperature plays a crucial role in manipulating solder successfully.

Generally, the larger the tip, the higher the iron temperature should be. If you want to retain detail in delicate beadwork, the iron temperature should be lower.

Once you've selected an iron, you'll want to select tips to use with it. Different tips are best suited to specific tasks (see below). Remember to clean iron tips often by wiping them on a tinning block while they are hot. Use these suggested iron settings as guidelines when beginning, and adjust as necessary:

(a) $1/8$" (3 mm) flat: Set iron to 80 watts. Use for delicate or small seams.

(b) $1/4$" (6 mm) flat: Set iron to 80 watts. Use for all-purpose work.

(c) $3/8$" (10 mm) flat: Set iron to 100 watts. Use for wide or large seams and outside box corners. (not shown)

(d) Grooved: Set iron to 80 watts. Use to create more rounded, raised beads. (not shown)

(e) Bent: Set iron to 80 watts. Use to make small, decorative accents or to make designs or indents in a larger bead.

Each soldering tip performs a special function.

COMBINING GLASS
WITH WOOD, METAL, AND NATURAL OBJECTS

One of the most exciting ways to enhance a stained glass work is to incorporate unexpected elements. Everyone knows—or thinks they know—what to expect when they hear the words "stained glass." But this art form, though ancient and traditional, doesn't have to be predictable.

An antique silver brooch, polished gemstones, shells, and even driftwood are just a few of the things that can be successfully joined with glass. So many effects can be achieved by mixing media—both striking and subtle, and always interesting. Imagine the warm, grainy texture of wood combined with a smooth piece of swirling green glass, or a polished burgundy-colored gem surrounded by similar but lighter shades of glass.

Trial and error is one sure way to discover how best to assemble a mixed media piece—but in this chapter, you'll learn a few simple principles and techniques that will help you to create beautiful and functional art right from the start. Once you start mixing and matching, nothing's safe from the soldering iron. Be inspired to stretch the boundaries of stained glass art and make a few discoveries of your own.

Mermaid Mirror

Imagine this dreamy, mist-covered mirror adorning a bathroom wall—a perfect seashell at the top adding a delightful, unexpected accent. This shell is stained pink; some shells are polished like gemstones to reveal a gorgeous array of shimmering natural tones. Choose glass that complements colors in the shell, or use sea-inspired blues. The opalescent pink glass used here suggests the delicate sheen often found inside shells.

MATERIALS

- Basic tools and supplies (see page 8)

- $1/2$ sheet of glass (6" x 12" or 15 cm x 30 cm) pearlescent or opalescent

- Seashell

- Uncoated picture-hanging wire

- Wire cutters

DESIGNER'S TIP

Choose shells that have at least one flat side so that the mirror will hang against a wall nicely. The areas of the shell to be foiled should also be fairly uniform in thickness to ensure a secure and even bond; shells can also be minimally and gently grozed, if necessary.

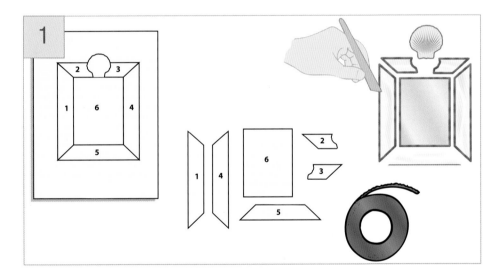

1. CUT AND FOIL THE GLASS PIECES. Prepare the pattern pieces and template (see page 285). Adjust the pattern as needed to accommodate the uniqueness of the selected shell. Score and break the glass as close as possible to the edge of the pattern pieces. Place the glass pieces on the corresponding areas of the template. Groze the edges of the glass for a snug fit, using the template as a guide. Then, foil the edges of each glass piece and the shell, making sure to center the glass edge on the foil, so that there is an even overlap on each side. Burnish the foiled areas.

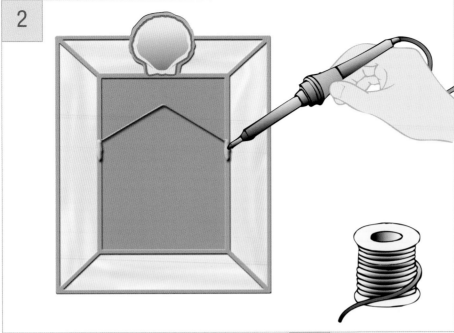

2. TACK THE SEAMS AND WIRE HANGER, THEN TIN ALL FOILED EDGES.
Arrange the foiled glass pieces on the template and use pushpins to keep them all snugly together. Brush flux on the foil at each point where the corners of the glass pieces meet. Use a small amount of solder to tack these areas together.

Add the wire hanger. Brush flux over the foiled edges. Unwind some solder from the roll. Use the tip of the iron to remove a little bit from the end of the solder strip, then run the iron over the foiled edges. Tin both the front and the back of the piece with a thin layer of solder. Be careful when turning the piece over, because the bonds will still be flexible.

Add the wire hanger. Cut a length of wire for the hanger. Brush flux on both ends of wire, covering $\frac{1}{4}$" (6 mm) (or more, if making a larger or heavier mirror than the one here). Fit the wire ends into the seams on both sides of the mirror, then remove and brush flux on these tinned areas. Tack the wire in place with a small amount of solder.

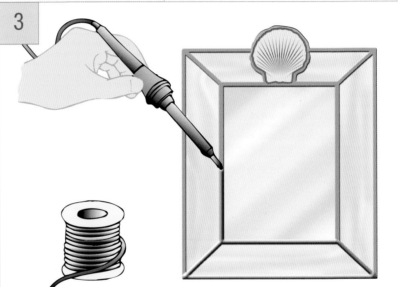

3. BEAD ALL TINNED AREAS.
Bead the piece using one of the methods described on page 14. Continue beading until all the seams are completed, and then let the piece cool completely before beading the other side. Reapply flux over tinned areas and beads in between each application of lead. If the project takes more than one day to complete, wash the piece and reapply the flux as needed.

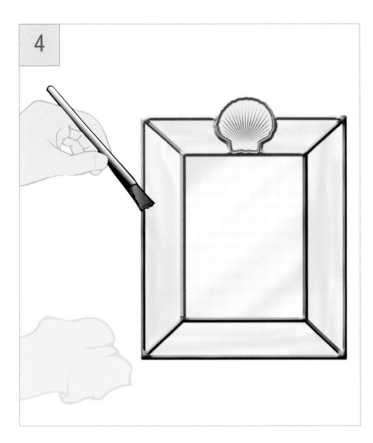

4

4. CLEAN AND FINISH THE PIECE. Once the piece has cooled, clean it with dishwashing liquid and a white sponge. Rinse well to remove all soapy residue. Dry completely with paper towels.

Apply patina of choice to the beaded areas (see page 15). Let the piece set for at least thirty minutes. Rinse with warm water and dry completely with paper towels again. Apply Simichrome polish in sparse dabs along the beaded areas, then buff gently with a soft cloth.

TRADE SECRETS

Scrap glass, which is normally destined for the trash, can be used to create a whole new work of art. It doesn't matter if they won't fit a pattern—try using them as is.

Save scraps from previous projects in clear plastic storage boxes, separated by color families. Then, lay several pieces on sturdy paper or cardboard, and play with the arrangement. Add more pieces, or take them away until something begins to take shape. This sort of project can't be predetermined; let the pieces inspire a design. Try beginning with one special piece, and then work around it.

Geode Candleholder

When geodes are first unearthed, they appear to be ordinary rocks—but once they are opened and polished, breathtaking colors and patterns are revealed. When cut thinly, like the slices used to make this candleholder, they become translucent. Test possible pieces for this project by holding them up to a candle flame; there will usually be areas of more or less translucency. Plan the positioning of the geode to accentuate the best areas.

MATERIALS

- Basic tools and supplies (see page 8)

- Right angle stand

- 1 full sheet of glass, not opaque (12" x 12" or 30 cm x 30 cm)

- Polished geode slices or other translucent gem-stones

DESIGNER'S TIP

Scrub the geode slices free of grime and sand using a toothbrush. Any particles trapped in the foil will eventually work themselves loose, even after beading.

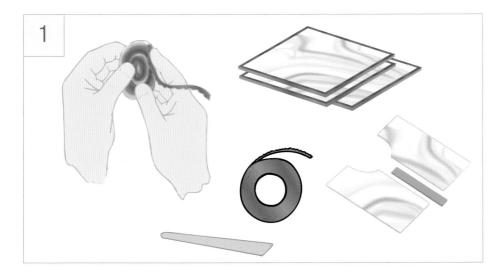

1. CUT AND FOIL THE GLASS PIECES. Prepare the pattern pieces and template (see page 286). Adjust the pattern as needed to accommodate the uniqueness of the selected geode slice. Score and break the glass as close as possible to the edge of the pattern pieces. Place the glass pieces on the corresponding areas of the template. Groze the edges of the glass for a snug fit, using the template as a guide. Then, foil the edges of each glass piece and the geode slice, making sure to center the glass edge on the foil, so that there is an even overlap on each side. Burnish the foiled areas.

2. TACK THE SEAMS, THEN TIN ALL FOILED EDGES.
Assemble the sides that have multiple pieces by brushing flux on the foil at the top and the bottom where the corners of the glass pieces meet. Use a small amount of solder to tack these areas together. Then, fit two sides of the candleholder into the right-angle holder, brush with flux at the top and the bottom where the corners of the glass pieces meet, and tack together. Add a third side in the same manner. Remove from the right-angle holder. Tack the fourth side in place. Then tack the bottom in place. Return the candleholder to the right-angle holder.

Brush flux over the foiled edges. Unwind some solder from the roll. Use the tip of the iron to remove a little bit from the end of the solder strip, then run the iron over the foiled edges. Tin all sides of the piece with a thin layer of solder. Be careful when handling the piece because the bonds will still be flexible.

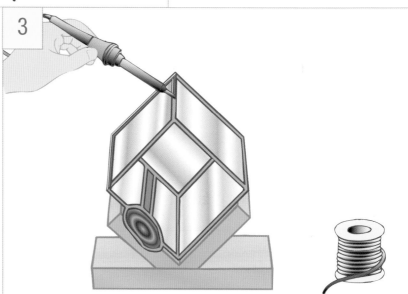

3. BEAD ALL TINNED AREAS. Touch the tip of the iron across the tinned seams. At the same time, position a strip of solder next to the tip of the iron. Move the iron slowly along the seam, allowing the solder to melt evenly along the foil. Continue beading until all the seams are completed, then turn the piece over and bead the other side. Reapply flux over tinned areas and beads in between each application of lead.

Wash the piece thoroughly with a white sponge and dishwashing detergent to remove all flux. If the project takes more than one day to complete, wash the piece and reapply the flux as needed.

TRADE SECRETS

Decorative metal objects, even delicate ones such as the antique metal butterfly on the candleholder shown with the main project, can be easily incorporated into a stained glass work.

To attach metal pieces to a project, either flux the piece directly or foil the edges. Brass, silver, and copper pieces can be directly soldered after applying flux, but alloys (such as white metal) typically can't. Another alternative is to wrap or affix wire to a piece of metal, and then solder the wire. Make sure the wire is uncoated, and be sure to apply flux.

4. CLEAN AND FINISH THE PIECE. Once the piece has cooled, clean it with dishwashing liquid and a white sponge. Rinse well to remove all soapy residue. Dry completely with paper towels.

Apply patina of choice to the beaded areas. Let the piece set for at least 30 minutes. Rinse with warm water and dry completely with paper towels again. Apply Simichrome polish in sparse dabs along the beaded areas, then buff gently with a soft cloth.

Trinket Tray

This small tray is the ideal holder for small pieces of jewelry, like rings or necklaces, but the pattern could easily be enlarged to make a serving tray. The free-form carved handles, which were made especially for this piece, echo the curving patterns in the glass. Try your hand at carving a set of handles, or choose pieces of wood, such as twigs, and work with the natural shape. For a completely different look, try using dowels or store-bought drawer pulls.

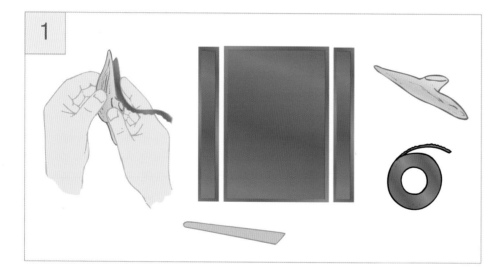

1. CUT THE GLASS AND FOIL ALL PIECES. Prepare the pattern pieces and template (see page 288). Adjust the pattern as needed to compensate for the uniqueness of the selected wood. Score and break the glass as close as possible to the edge of the pattern pieces. Place the glass pieces on the corresponding areas of the template. Groze the edges of the glass for a snug fit, using the template as a guide. Then, foil the edges of each glass piece and the wood, making sure to center the glass edge on the foil, so that there is an even overlap on each side. Use wide foil for the wood pieces to ensure that the soldered seam will be big enough to handle the stress of use. Burnish the foiled areas.

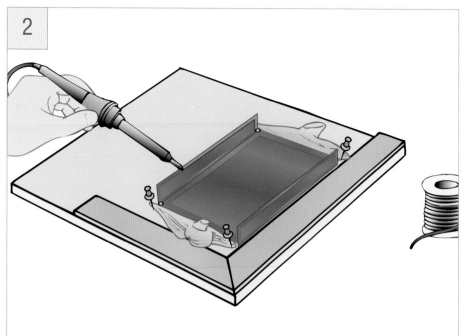

2. TACK THE SEAMS, AND THEN TIN ALL FOILED EDGES.
Position the bottom and sides of the tray against the
table brace, and use pushpins to hold everything
together. Brush flux on the foil at each point where
the corners of the glass pieces meet. Use a small
amount of solder to tack these areas together.

Brush flux over the foiled edges. Unwind some solder
from the roll. Use the tip of the iron to remove a little
bit from the end of the solder strip, and then run the
iron over the foiled edges. Tin all seams with a thin
layer of solder. Be careful when handling the piece
because the bonds will still be flexible. Once cool,
turn the piece over and tin the bottom.

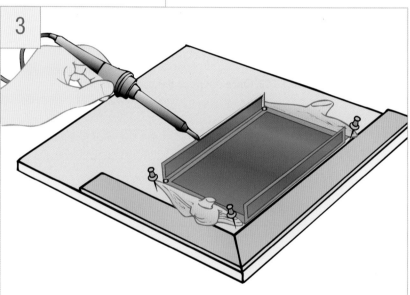

3. BEAD ALL TINNED AREAS. Bead the piece using one of the methods
described on page 14. Continue beading until all the seams are
completed, and then let the piece cool completely before beading
the other side. Reapply flux over tinned areas and beads in between
each application of lead. If the project takes more than one day to
complete, wash the piece and reapply the flux as needed.

Wood is easily scorched by the heat of soldering irons, so use caution when assembling your project. Keep in mind that harder woods such as oak or maple won't scorch as easily as pine and other soft woods. Of course, softer woods can be used with care, and wood-burned accents could add to a rustic look.

Experiment with incorporating store-bought wood trims or appliqués with glass; the usually traditional designs of such items will lend a classic appeal to a project. A lacy, open appliqué could be used to make the perfect focal point for the top of an old-fashioned potpourri container.

4. CLEAN AND FINISH THE PIECE. Once the piece has cooled, clean it with dishwashing liquid and a white sponge. Rinse well to remove all soapy residue. Dry completely with paper towels.

Apply patina of choice to the beaded areas (see page 15). Let the piece set for at least thirty minutes. Rinse with warm water and dry completely with paper towels again. Apply Simichrome polish in sparse dabs along the beaded areas, and then buff gently with a soft cloth.

DECORATIVE
SURFACE TECHNIQUES

The beauty of glass can be further enhanced with surface decorating techniques such as painting, etching, and engraving. These techniques allow the artist to truly personalize a piece; the potential for self-statement increases exponentially with the addition of these simple skills to your repertoire.

Painted details can be kiln fired, oven baked, or air dried, giving the modern glass artist a variety of colors and effects from which to choose. Etching, in contrast, works by removing the surface layer of glass, producing a matte effect. It is an intriguing and often subtle way to enhance your work. Etched designs are created using stencils, which you can purchase or design yourself using adhesive vinyl. Experiment with the interplay between etched and unetched surfaces, which will affect the way a piece diffuses light dramatically. Engraving tools produce a similar matte effect; they allow you to draw designs on glass, which is particularly appealing. These tools aren't simply for signing your name!

More advanced techniques for surface decoration include sandblasting and kiln-fired painting. You'll see some beautiful examples of these techniques in the Gallery of Art Glass, which begins on page 86.

Tulip Vase

The tulip on this elegant, functional vase was cut so that the streaks in the glass are positioned vertically, which is reminiscent of how real petals would unfold. The addition of a painted highlight at the top completes the effect of a blossoming tulip. Simple but effective, the painted accents were created using glass stains specially formulated for stained glass work. The stains hold up to handling and washing and will remain glossy without being heat set.

MATERIALS

- Basic tools and supplies (see page 8)

- 1 full sheet of pale yellow glass (12" x 12" or 30 cm x 30 cm)

- Scrap of glass for tulip, medium yellow

- Color Magic glass stains (see Resources, page 299)

- Paintbrush

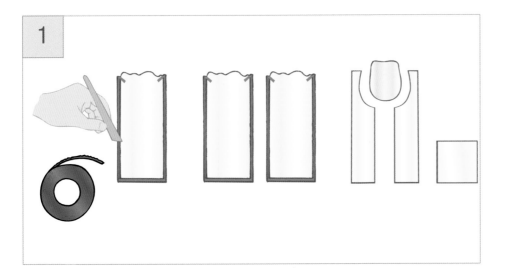

DESIGNER'S TIP

This vase has small feet, which are made by melting a little extra solder and allowing it to pool at each corner seam. Practice this technique on scraps first, making sure that the seam is perpendicular to a level work surface.

1. CUT AND FOIL THE GLASS PIECES. Prepare the pattern pieces and template (see page 289). Score and break the glass as close as possible to the edge of the pattern pieces. Place the glass pieces on the corresponding areas of the template. Groze the edges of the glass for a snug fit, using the template as a guide. Then, foil the edges of each glass, making sure to center the glass edge on the foil, so that there is an even overlap on each side. Burnish the foiled areas. The top edges of this vase were left unfoiled. See Trade Secrets on page 35.

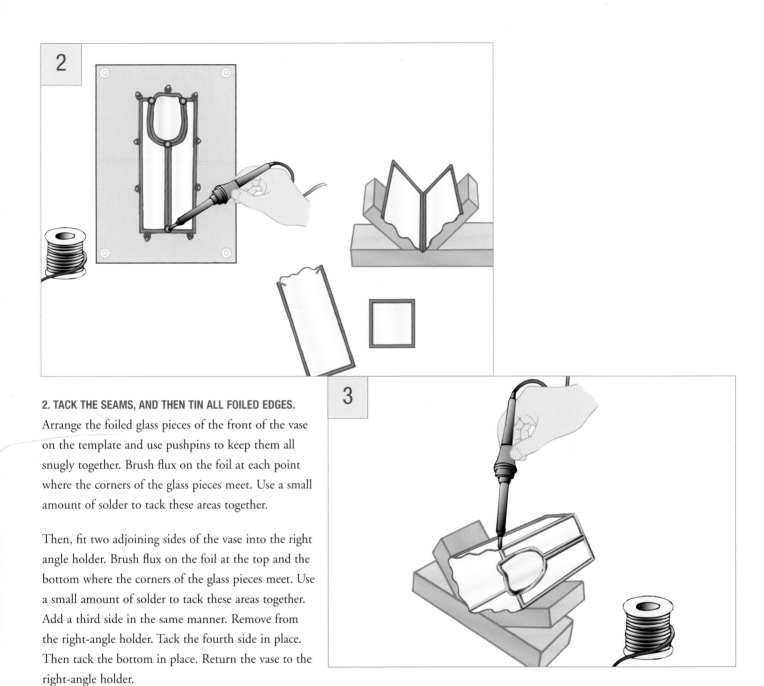

2. TACK THE SEAMS, AND THEN TIN ALL FOILED EDGES.
Arrange the foiled glass pieces of the front of the vase
on the template and use pushpins to keep them all
snugly together. Brush flux on the foil at each point
where the corners of the glass pieces meet. Use a small
amount of solder to tack these areas together.

Then, fit two adjoining sides of the vase into the right
angle holder. Brush flux on the foil at the top and the
bottom where the corners of the glass pieces meet. Use
a small amount of solder to tack these areas together.
Add a third side in the same manner. Remove from
the right-angle holder. Tack the fourth side in place.
Then tack the bottom in place. Return the vase to the
right-angle holder.

Brush flux over the foiled edges. Unwind some solder from the
roll. Use the tip of the iron to remove a little bit from the end of
the solder strip, and then run the iron over the foiled edges. Tin
both the inside and outside of the piece with a thin layer of solder. Be careful when handling the piece because the bonds will
still be flexible.

3. BEAD ALL TINNED AREAS. Place the vase in the right-angle holder
with a seam parallel to the work surface. Bead the piece using one
of the methods described on page 14. Continue beading until all
the seams are completed, and then place the piece on the work surface and bead the top and inside bottom seams, which will be parallel to the work surface. Reapply flux over tinned areas and beads
in between each application of lead. If the project takes more than
one day to complete, wash the piece and reapply the flux as needed.

Once the piece has cooled, clean it with dishwashing liquid and a
white sponge. Rinse well to remove all soapy residue. Dry completely with paper towels.

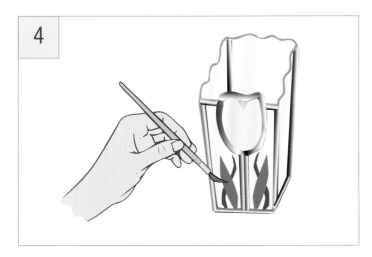

4

4. PAINT ACCENTS AND FINISH THE PIECE. Apply patina of choice to the beaded areas (see page 15). Let the piece set for at least thirty minutes. Rinse with warm water and dry completely with paper towels again. Apply Simichrome polish in sparse dabs along the beaded areas, and then buff
gently with a soft cloth.

Paint the leaves and the tulip highlight. Practice painting on pieces of scrap glass first to get a feel for how the stains work. As with most glass paints, stains have a limited workability time, so practice brush strokes and try to minimize the amount needed to achieve the desired effect. It's also helpful to experiment with brushes of different sizes and shapes. Color Magic glass stains can also be used on solder; the tulip stem here was painted with green stain that was then wiped off, creating a subtle wash of color.

TRADE SECRETS
The top edges of the sides and back of this vase are not foiled. Rather, the natural free-form edge of the glass sheet is used as is. This adds an additional element of interest and works wonderfully in a piece with a nature-inspired theme. Choose a glass sheet that doesn't have chips or sharp areas on the edge.

Try this easy technique for an attractive bead when partially foiling a piece: Leave tails of extra foil approximately 1/4" (6 mm) past the edge of the seams adjacent to the unfoiled areas. Tin the excess along with the rest of the seams. When beading the seams, allow the bead to extend to this tail, but don't worry about making it look good. Then, trim the excess neatly with a craft knife and burnish the edge.

The natural edge of a glass
sheet inspired this compostition.

Art Deco Napkin Holder

The geometric shape combined with the silver and black color scheme of this napkin holder is reminiscent of Art Deco designs, which is an artistic style that began in the 1920s. Dragonflies were also a popular motif used by Art Deco artisans. The unbroken surface of this piece is the perfect place to add an etched detail, like the dragonfly seen here. Consult art history or clip art books for other decorative motifs in this style.

MATERIALS

- Basic tools and supplies (see page 8)

- ¹/₂ sheet of black glass (6" x 12" or 15 cm x 30 cm)

- Scrap of white glass for base

- Clear adhesive vinyl

- Etchall glass etching creme

- Etchall squeegee applicator

- Etchall swivel knife

- Rubber gloves

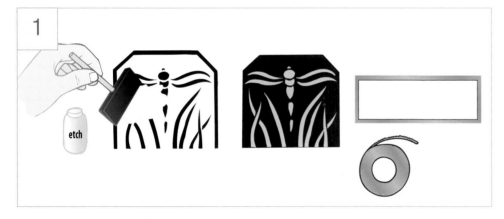

1. CUT, ETCH, AND FOIL THE GLASS PIECES. Prepare the pattern pieces and template (see page 290). Score and break the glass as close as possible to the edge of the pattern pieces. Place the glass pieces on the corresponding areas of the template.

Photocopy the etching pattern on page 290. Cut out the black areas to make a stencil; trace this outline on a piece of adhesive vinyl using a permanent marker. Use a swivel craft knife to carefully cut the pattern out of the vinyl. Firmly press the vinyl pattern to the glass. Following the manufacturer's directions, apply a thick, even layer of creme to the glass with a squeegee applicator. Wait five minutes, and then use the applicator to scrape off as much of the creme as possible and put it back in the bottle. Rinse off the remaining creme under warm running water, and remove the vinyl pattern. Be sure to wear rubber gloves when working with etching creme.

Groze the edges of the glass for a snug fit, using the template as a guide. Then, foil the edges of each glass piece, making sure to center the glass edge on the foil, so that there is an even overlap on each side. Burnish the foiled areas.

DESIGNER'S TIP

Scalloped copper foil was used on the bottom edge of this piece. When foiling edges that will be joined with another piece of glass at a 90-degree angle, be sure that at least 1/8" (3 mm) of foil covers the inside edges to ensure a sturdy seam.

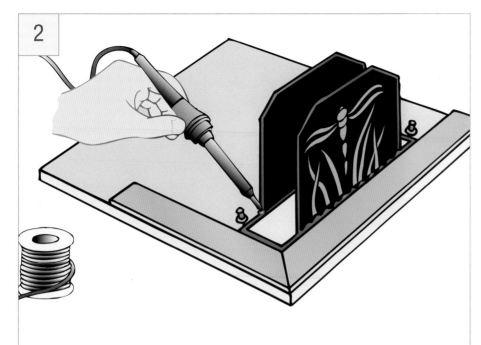

2. TACK THE SEAMS, AND THEN TIN ALL FOILED EDGES.

Position one side of the napkin holder against the right edge of the table brace. Position the bottom of the holder so that it is against and centered along this side of the napkin holder. Slide the pieces into the corner, so that the short edge of the bottom piece is snug against the bottom brace. Position the other side and use pushpins to hold everything in place. Brush flux on the foil at each point where the corners of the glass pieces meet. Use a small amount of solder to tack these areas together.

Brush flux over the foiled edges. Unwind some solder from the roll. Use the tip of the iron to remove a little bit from the end of the solder strip, and then run the iron over the foiled edges. Tin all seams with a thin layer of solder. Be careful when handling the piece because the bonds will still be flexible. Once the piece is cool, turn it over and tin the bottom.

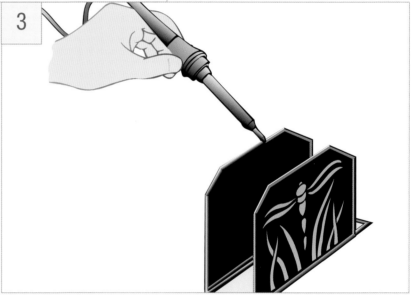

3. BEAD ALL TINNED AREAS.
Bead the piece using one of the methods described on page 14. Continue beading until all the seams are completed, and then let the piece cool completely before beading the other side. Reapply flux over tinned areas and beads in between each application of lead. If the project takes more than one day to complete, wash the piece and reapply the flux as needed.

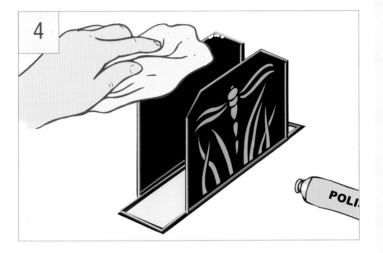

4. CLEAN AND FINISH THE PIECE. Once the piece has cooled, clean it with dishwashing liquid and a white sponge. Rinse well to remove all soapy residue. Dry completely with paper towels.

Apply patina of choice to the beaded areas (see page 15). Let the piece set for at least thirty minutes. Rinse with warm water and dry completely with paper towels again. Apply Simichrome polish in sparse dabs along the beaded areas, and then buff gently with a soft cloth.

TRADE SECRETS

Glass etching is a wonderful way to add surface designs to stained glass—the interplay between matte and shiny surfaces can be bold or subtle, depending on the glass chosen. Etching on black glass creates the most contrast—the result indeed looks frosted.

When planning an etched design, test the etching creme on the selected glass. In general, the darker the glass, the more visible the etching will be, but also consider where the item will be displayed. If the piece will be blasted by natural light, the etching will probably be barely noticeable. An indoor setting with mostly indirect but bright light will usually show off the design best.

Sandblasting produces an effect similar to etching, but results in a reverse-relief. The white-on-white design creates an ethereal look.

Mooncatcher

You've seen suncatchers in gift stores that abound in sunny locales. Why not make a moon-catcher like the one seen here? An etched design on deep blue glass creates a mysterious, moody look befitting the moon. Finely engraved details add more depth to the etched area, giving this moon character. Try cutting a crescent-shaped piece of glass, or assembling small stars. Hang them all together in a window for a lovely mobile effect.

MATERIALS

• Basic stained glass tools and supplies (see page 8)

• 1/2 sheet of cobalt glass, 6" x 12" (15 cm x 30 cm)

• Adhesive vinyl

• Etchall glass etching creme

• Etchall squeegee applicator

• Etchall swivel knife

• Rubber gloves

• Engraving tool

• 20-gauge copper wire

• Wire cutters

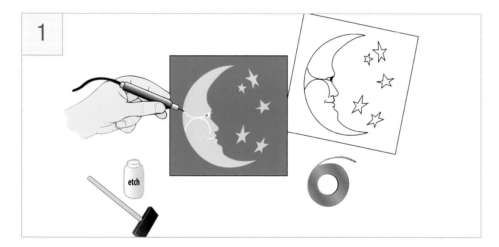

1. CUT, ETCH, AND FOIL THE GLASS PIECE. Prepare the pattern piece and template (see page 291). Score and break the glass as closely as possible to the edge of the pattern piece. Place the glass piece on the corresponding area of the template.

Photocopy the etching pattern on page 291. Cut out the black areas to make a stencil; trace this outline on a piece of adhesive vinyl using a permanent marker. Use a swivel craft knife to carefully cut the pattern out of the vinyl. Firmly press the vinyl pattern to the glass. Following the manufacturer's directions, use the creme to etch the glass. Be sure to wear rubber gloves when working with etching creme. Accentuate the facial features in the design as desired using an engraving tool (see Trade Secrets, page 43). Groze the edges of the glass for a snug fit, using the template as a guide. Then, foil the edges of each glass piece, making sure to center the glass edge on the foil, so that there is an even overlap on each side. Burnish the foiled areas.

DESIGNER'S TIP

Try using permanent marker over engraved lines to highlight certain areas. The mouth and eye on the piece seen here were highlighted using a black marker.

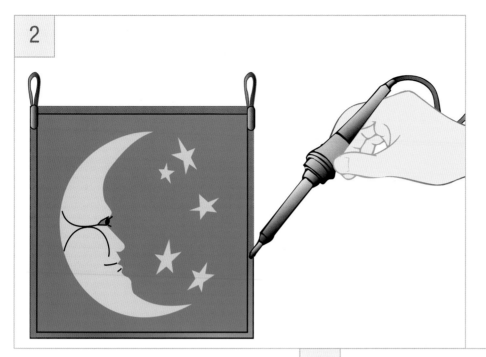

2. TACK THE HANGERS IN PLACE AND TIN ALL FOILED EDGES. Twist the copper wire into loops to create the hangers. Brush flux on the loops and the topside edges of the mooncatcher. Use a small amount of solder to tack the loops in place.

Brush flux over the foiled edges. Unwind some solder from the roll. Use the tip of the iron to remove a little bit from the end of the solder strip, and then run the iron over the foiled edges. Tin all seams with a thin layer of solder. Once cool, turn the piece over and tin the back.

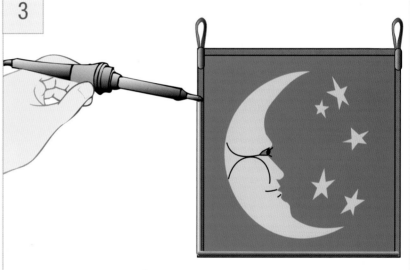

3. BEAD ALL TINNED AREAS. Bead the piece using one of the methods described on page 14. Continue beading until all the seams are completed, and then let the piece cool completely before beading the other side. Reapply flux over tinned areas and beads in between each application of lead. If the project takes more than one day to complete, wash the piece and reapply the flux as needed.

4. CLEAN AND FINISH THE PIECE. Once the piece has cooled, clean it with dishwashing liquid and a white sponge. Rinse well to remove all soapy residue. Dry completely with paper towels.

Apply patina of choice to the beaded areas (see page 15). Let the piece set for at least thirty minutes. Rinse with warm water and dry completely with paper towels again. Apply Simichrome polish in sparse dabs along the beaded areas, and then buff gently with a soft cloth.

TRADE SECRETS

Engraving tools are inexpensive and very simple to use. The diamond-coated tip lightly carves glass, leaving a white line on any color of glass.

Hold the tool as you would a pencil or paintbrush. You can control the thickness of the lines by applying more or less pressure. For a very fine line, just barely graze the surface of the glass. Try to maintain the amount of pressure to create a line of consistent thickness. Don't draw over the same line too many times, as this will cause the glass to chip.

CREATIVE
FOILING AND BEADWORK

Often overlooked are the humble foil and solder that keep stained glass works together, but just because these seams are necessary doesn't mean they have to look utilitarian. In fact, soldering can be the focal point of a piece and is always a crucial part of any overall design. After you've learned how to construct a simple, elegant bead, it's time to explore.

One easy way to spice up your soldered lines is to use scalloped foil. Foil also comes in different sizes; take advantage of this by creating seams of various widths in the same piece. Thicker lines will accentuate an area, attracting the viewer's eye. Or, skip the seams altogether, and try decoratively cutting foil and adhering it to the surface of glass, as in the Tree Tea Light project on page 54.

Even if your foiled seams are straightforward, you can add texture to your beadwork by sculpting solder. See Iron Tips and Temperatures on page 15 for advice on how to manipulate solder effectively, and you'll be well on your way to on creating striking dimensional beads.

Cabochon Jewelry Box

The leopard skin jasper cabochon that adorns this box is characterized by swirls and dots of beautiful, earthy colors. The voluptuous beadwork that surrounds it was inspired by the patterns inherent in the stone. Design a box like this one by first selecting a stone. Bring the stone along when selecting glass, and choose pieces that match the more subtle colors in the rock. This will visually draw out and enhance the natural patterns.

MATERIALS

- Basic stained glass tools and supplies (see page 8)

- Right-angle holder

- 1 full sheet of glass or different pieces to equal 1 full sheet, 12" x 12" (30 cm x 30 cm)

- Polished gemstone cabochon, washed and dried

- Jewelry chain

- Brass tube and wire set for box making (see Resources, page 299)

- Brass ball feet (optional)

- Hobby saw

- Wire cutters

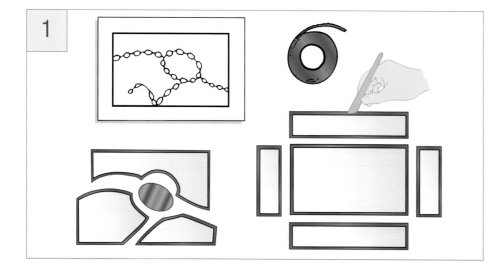

1. CUT AND FOIL THE GLASS PIECES. Prepare the pattern pieces and template (see page 292). Adjust the pattern as needed to compensate for the uniqueness of the selected gemstone cabochon. Score and break the glass as closely as possible to the edge of the pattern pieces. Place the glass pieces on the corresponding areas of the template. Groze the edges of the glass for a snug fit, using the template as a guide. Then, foil the edges of each glass piece and the cabochon, making sure to center the glass edge on the foil, so that there is an even overlap on each side. Burnish the foiled areas.

DESIGNER'S TIP

Add ball feet to a box to give it a special touch. Simply apply flux to the feet and the bottom of the box where they will be attached, and then tack and solder in place.

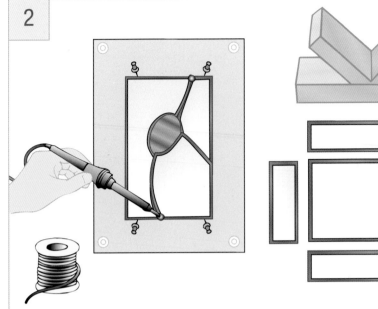

2. TACK THE SEAMS, AND THEN TIN ALL FOILED EDGES.

Arrange the foiled glass pieces of box top on the
template and use pushpins to keep them all snugly
together. Brush flux on the foil at each point where
the corners of the glass pieces meet. Use a small
amount of solder to tack these areas together. Set
the top aside.

Then, fit two adjoining sides of the box base into the
right-angle holder. Brush flux on the foil at the top
and the bottom where the corners of the glass pieces
meet. Use a small amount of solder to tack these areas
together. Add a third side in the same manner.
Remove from the right-angle holder. Tack the fourth
side in place. Then tack the bottom in place. Return
the box to the right-angle holder.

Brush flux over the foiled edges. Unwind some solder from the
roll. Use the tip of the iron to remove a little bit from the end of
the solder strip, and then run the iron over the foiled edges. Tin
both the inside and outside of the box base and the separate box
top with a thin layer of solder. Be careful when handling the box
because the bonds will still be flexible.

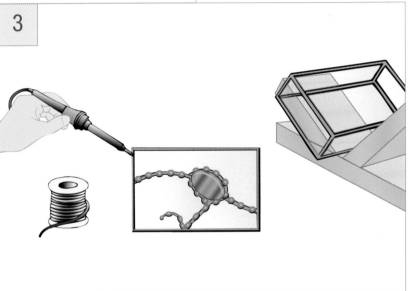

3. BEAD ALL TINNED AREAS.

Place the box base in the right-angle
holder with a seam parallel to the work surface. Bead the piece
using one of the methods described on page 14. Continue beading
until all the seams are completed, but leave the two back inside
corner seams simply tinned; this is where the box top attachments
will be made. Then, place the piece on the work surface and bead
the other three top seams, which will be parallel to the work surface.
Also bead the box top, leaving the back edge simply tinned.

Reapply flux over tinned areas and beads in between each application of lead. If the project takes more than one day to complete,
wash the piece and reapply the flux as needed.

Once the piece has cooled, clean it with dishwashing liquid
and a white sponge. Rinse well to remove all soapy residue.
Dry completely with paper towels.

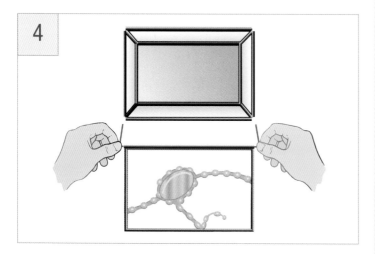

4. ATTACH THE BOX TOP AND FINISH THE PIECE. Using a hobby saw, trim the brass tube $\frac{1}{4}$" (6 mm) to $\frac{1}{2}$" (1 cm) shorter than the back edge of box top. Center the tube along the back edge of the box top and use pushpins to secure both to the work surface. Brush flux on the tube and the edge of the box top, and then tack, tin, and bead the seam. Next, cut a piece of the brass wire and thread it through the tube, so that it extends out of the tube about 1" (2.5 cm) at both ends. Place the box top on the box base. Bend the 1" (2.5 cm) wire ends outside the box, nestling them in the outside corner seams. Tack, tin, and then bead over the wires.

Use wire cutters to trim a piece of jewelry chain obviously longer than needed. Flux 1" (2.5 cm) of the chain end and a beaded seam close to one side on the box top, about 1" (2.5 cm) down from what will be the front (opening) edge. Tack and solder the chain in place. Hold the top open as much as you want, and then trim the chain leaving $\frac{1}{2}$" (1 cm) extra. Nestle the chain inside the corner of the box directly below where the chain is attached to the box top. Tack and solder the chain in place.

Apply patina of choice to the beaded areas (see page 15). Let the piece set for at least thirty minutes. Rinse with warm water and dry completely with paper towels again. Apply Simichrome polish in sparse dabs along the beaded areas, and then buff gently with a soft cloth.

TRADE SECRETS

The beadwork on this box has much more dimension than a standard semicircular bead. The secret to successful dimensional beadwork is to melt off small pieces of solder, position them on seams, and then dab the edges to secure. Try to minimize melting, rather completely melting the solder as in the traditional method.

When working on a long seam, work in small sections. Let beads cool enough so that they haze over, about a minute or so, and then continue along the seam. This will lessen the chance of accidentally melting the previous bead.

Bird in Flight

This panel incorporates both straight and scalloped foil. Combining these shapes is an easy way to incorporate interesting beadwork into a piece. When planning a design, carefully consider where to place the seams. The ruffled bead near the shell here suggests downy feathers, but when the rippled edges extend into the space around the bird, they suggest movement, air currents, and clouds. The straight beads continue the line of the beak and tail gracefully, adding to the fluidity of the design.

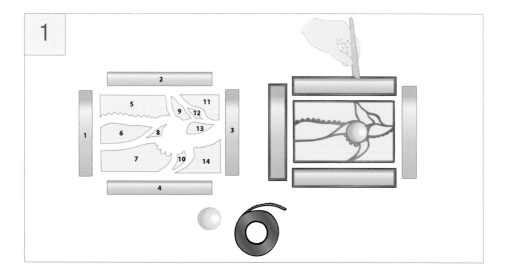

1. CUT AND FOIL THE GLASS PIECES. Prepare the pattern pieces and template (see page 293). Adjust the pattern as needed to compensate for the uniqueness of the selected shell. Score and break the glass as closely as possible to the edge of the pattern pieces. Place the glass pieces on the corresponding areas of the template. Groze the edges of the glass for a snug fit, using the template as a guide. Then foil the edges of each glass piece and the shell, making sure to center the glass edge on the foil, so that there is an even overlap on each side. Burnish the foiled areas.

MATERIALS

- Basic stained glass tools and supplies (see page 8)

- 1 full sheet of glass or different pieces to equal 1 full sheet, 12" x 12" (30 cm x 30 cm)

- Seashell

- Sturdy chain for hanging

- Copper channel framing (optional)

- Craft knife

- Wire cutters

DESIGNER'S TIP

To frame a piece with the copper channel seen here, cut a strip about 2" (5 cm) longer than needed to encompass the panel. Wrap the channel around the panel, notching the corners with a craft knife so they overlap neatly. Trim the excess, and then flux and solder the ends at one corner.

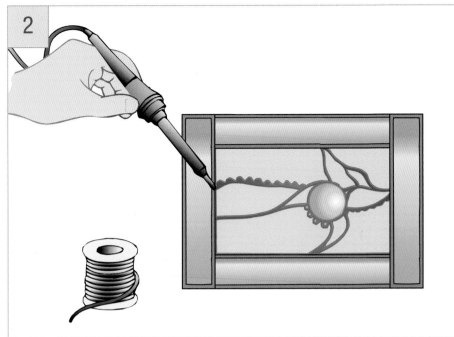

2. TACK THE SEAMS, AND THEN TIN ALL FOILED EDGES.

Arrange the foiled glass pieces on the template and use pushpins to keep them snugly together. Brush flux on the foil at each point where the corners of the glass pieces meet. Use a small amount of solder to tack these areas together.

Brush flux over the foiled edges. Unwind some solder from the roll. Use the tip of the iron to remove a little bit from the end of the solder strip, and then run the iron over the foiled edges. Tin both the front and the back of the piece with a thin layer of solder. Be careful when turning the piece over because the bonds will still be flexible.

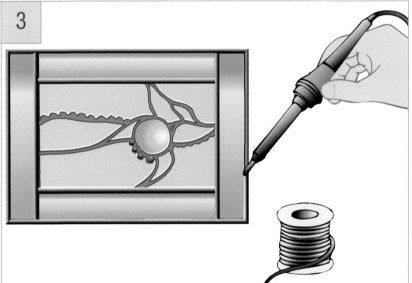

3. BEAD ALL TINNED AREAS. Bead the piece using one of the methods described on page 14. Continue beading until all the seams are completed, and then let the piece cool completely before beading the other side. Reapply flux over tinned areas and beads in between each application of lead. If the project takes more than one day to complete, wash the piece and reapply the flux as needed.

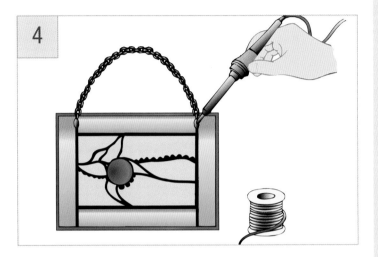

4

4. CLEAN AND FINISH THE PIECE. Once the piece has cooled, clean it with dishwashing liquid and a white sponge. Rinse well to remove all soapy residue. Dry completely with paper towels.

Apply patina of choice to the beaded areas (see page 15). Let the piece set for at least thirty minutes. Rinse with warm water and dry completely with paper towels again. Apply Simichrome polish in sparse dabs along the beaded areas, and then buff gently with a soft cloth.

Attach the chain for hanging by cutting a length of chain. Flux 1" (2.5 cm) of the chain ends and the vertical beaded seams on the left and right sides of the panel, beginning just under the copper channel, if framing the piece (see Designer's Tip on page 51). Tack and solder the chain in place.

TRADE SECRETS

Beaded accents can be built up by adding successive layers of solder. To do this, it's imperative to let each layer of solder cool completely to the touch. Add the next layer quickly, and let it cool again. If you make a mistake, wait until the layer has cooled to fix it. Applying heat for too long will melt all previous layers.

To create a rippled or "combed" bead, set the soldering iron to a low or medium setting. Then, gently push ripples into a rounded bead. The lower temperature allows more time to shape the solder without melting it completely.

Tree Tea Light

This elegant tree design is created entirely of foil and solder. When a solid design such as this one is layered on translucent glass, light is cast around the image so that it seems to glow, creating a romantic, ethereal mood. To create the dimensional look of this tree, first build up layers of solder, and then use a cool iron to give the tree barklike details. See Iron Tips and Temperature on page 15, and Trade Secrets on page 57 for information on sculpting solder.

MATERIALS

- Basic stained glass tools and supplies (see page 8)

- ½ sheet of translucent glass, 6" x 12" (15 cm x 30 cm)

- 3 scraps of glass for the base

DESIGNER'S TIP

Try using a heavily textured glass, which diffuses light in interesting and often unusual ways, to make candleholders. The glass used here has deep linear ridges on the back.

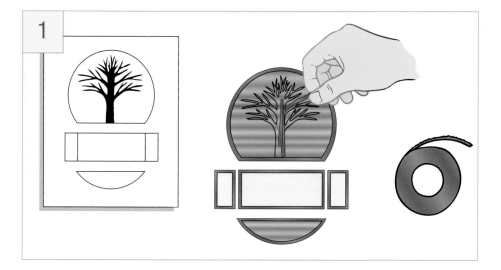

1. CUT AND FOIL THE GLASS PIECES. Prepare the pattern pieces and template (see page 294). Score and break the glass as closely as possible to the edge of the pattern pieces. Place the glass pieces on the corresponding areas of the template.

Groze the edges of the glass for a snug fit, using the template as a guide. Then, foil the edges of each glass piece, making sure to center the glass edge on the foil so that there is an even overlap on each side. Burnish the foiled areas. Create the tree design by burnishing foil on the front piece of the holder (see Trade Secrets, page 57).

2. TACK THE SEAMS, AND THEN TIN ALL FOILED EDGES.

Position the pieces for the base of the holder against the table brace and use pushpins to hold everything in place. Brush flux on the foil at each point where the corners of the glass pieces meet. Use a small amount of solder to tack these areas together. Align the front of the holder against the table brace. Position the base and the back piece against the front piece and use pushpins to hold everything in place. Flux and tack the piece together.

Brush flux over the foiled edges. Unwind some solder from the roll. Use the tip of the iron to remove a little bit from the end of the solder strip, and then run the iron over the foiled edges. Tin all seams with a thin layer of solder. Be careful when handling the piece because the bonds will still be flexible. Once the piece is cool, turn it over and tin the bottom.

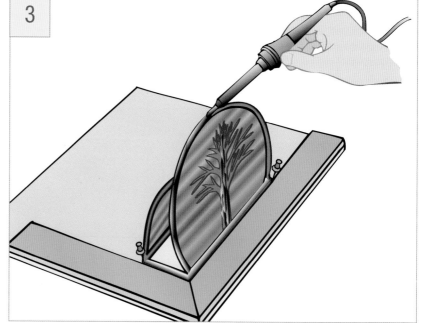

3. BEAD ALL TINNED AREAS. Bead the piece using one of the methods described on page 14. Continue beading until all the seams are completed, and then let the piece cool completely before beading the other side. Build up layers of solder to create a dimensional look, if desired. Reapply flux over tinned areas and beads in between each application of lead. If the project takes more than one day to complete, wash the piece and reapply the flux as needed.

4. CLEAN AND FINISH THE PIECE. Once the piece has cooled, clean it with dishwashing liquid and a white sponge. Rinse well to remove all soapy residue. Dry completely with paper towels.

Apply patina of choice to the beaded areas (see page 15). Let the piece set for at least thirty minutes. Rinse with warm water and dry completely with paper towels again. Apply Simichrome polish in sparse dabs along the beaded areas, and then buff gently with a soft cloth.

TRADE SECRETS

To create a superficial soldered design, split and shape wide foil with a craft knife as you adhere it to the surface of the glass. The pieces should be 1" (2.5 cm) or longer to ensure durability. Also experiment with scalloped foil and different widths. To prevent the design from peeling away from the glass, be sure to secure the ends of the foil around the bottom or side edges of the glass.

It's easy to create your own unique designs; simply sketch or trace a line drawing of the desired image. Then, slip the drawing under the glass to use as a guideline.

WARM GLASS
BASIC TECHNIQUES

GETTING STARTED

There are only a few supplies you'll need to get started; they are described in the following list.

When setting up your work space, the most important consideration is the kiln. Be sure to keep it out of the reach of children, pets, and flammable material; make sure there is adequate ventilation; and make sure the electrical outlet is equipped to conduct the amount of energy required by the kiln. Read the owner's manual thoroughly, as this contains all the specific information you'll need to ensure safety.

Photo courtesy of Skutt Kilns.

BASIC FUSED GLASS TOOLS AND SUPPLIES

01. A *fusing glass kiln* is the most expensive and important piece of equipment needed for warm glass techniques. Though ceramic kilns can be used, it's best to purchase a kiln designed for fusing. Kilns are carefully calibrated instruments, and you'll get the best results from a kiln designed to suit your purpose.

02. *Kiln wash and kiln paper* are used to protect the interior surfaces of the kiln from the fusing glass. Without this separating layer, glass would stick to the kiln. Kiln wash is applied wet and allowed to dry; kiln paper is therefore faster and easier. Be sure that the paper is intended for glass fusing kilns, so it won't burn.

03. *Kiln shelves and molds* are used to support glass during fusing and slumping. These accessories can be purchased from glass fusing and kiln suppliers. Stainless steel objects, such as mixing bowls, also make ideal molds for slumping.

04. The same *glass cutting tools and groziers* used for cold glass techniques can be used to cut and shape glass prior to fusing. See Basic Stained Glass Tools and Supplies on page 8.

05. *Safety equipment* such as rubber gloves and particle masks. Wear gloves when handling kiln paper, and wear a particle mask when mixing kiln wash. Of course, when cutting glass, be sure to where safety goggles (see Safety! Safety! Safety! on page 10).

SELECTING GLASS

Any glass can be used for warm glass techniques, however, glass specially formulated for fusing and slumping is much easier to work with because it is designed to give consistent, satisfactory results.

GLASS COMPATIBILITY

The beauty of fused pieces is usually due to unique and interesting combinations of glass. When planning glass combinations, you'll need to know whether the glass is compatible.

When glass is heated and cooled during the fusing process, it expands and contracts at a specific rate. If you use two pieces of glass with different expansion and contraction rates, the piece may crack—or worse, shatter—when the piece cools. This characteristic is referred to as the coefficient of expansion (COE).

Don't worry—you don't need to be a scientist to fuse glass. Manufacturers who sell glass for fusing test for compatibility, and list the COE of their product. For example, Spectrum System 96™ glass, made by Uroboros Glass, has a COE of 96. All of the glass in this product line is compatible with each other, making glass selection easy (see Resources on page 299).

TALKING GLASS

There are many kinds of glass to choose from; new glass formulas are always being developed. In addition, some types of glass have decorative coatings, which expands the palette even further. Below is a list of terms that are used to describe specific attributes of glass.

- **Cathedral glass** is simply translucent colored glass. Opaque glass is often referred to as **opalescent glass**.
- **Stained glass** used for cold techniques can also be used for fusing and is sometimes referred to as **art glass**.
- **Iridescent glass** is any glass that has been treated with an iridescent coating, which is only superficial. Keep in mind that when the piece is lit from behind, the iridescence won't be visible. Some coatings will burn off in the kiln, unless the glass is specially formulated for fusing.
- **Dichroic glass** is coated with a film that creates a special optical effect: The glass appears to be different colors when viewed at different angles. It is available in a range of color combinations, textures, and patterns.

BEYOND FLAT SHEET GLASS

Add texture to a project by experimenting with the various shapes and sizes of glass available from suppliers for warm glass techniques.

- *Rods* are round cylinders of glass that are available in various thicknesses. Try cutting them into slices to create "millefiore" designs.
- *Stringers* are thin threads of glass that can be softened and manipulated using the heat from a candle. Try weaving them to create a fabric texture.
- *Confetti* (also called shards) is very thin slices of glass that can be layered over other colors to paint designs.
- *Frit* refers to small, irregularly shaped glass pieces, ranging from powder to chunks. Sprinkle some over a project to add a colorful pattern.

TESTING GLASS COMPATIBILITY

Once you become comfortable with the fusing process, you will probably be itching to try glass beyond that sold for fusing. Try this simple test to discover how the glass you've chosen will hold up under pressure:

1. Fuse small pieces of the glass you would like to test, and then let the test sample cool completely. If the piece hasn't visibly cracked, this means the glass isn't totally incompatible. However, there may still be some stressed areas that aren't yet visible, but will eventually crack.

2. To test the piece further, place it in the freezer for twenty-four hours, and then remove and let it warm to room temperature. Any hidden stress points should reveal themselves.

3. Test the glass combination even further by running the fused sample though a dishwashing cycle. The cold of the freezer followed by the heat of the dishwasher is a great way to test durability; this is especially important for functional pieces that are intended for everyday use.

PREPARING THE KILN FOR FIRING

First and foremost, read the owner's manual. The manufacturer will guide you through the steps in setting up your particular kiln. Generally, you will have to perform a test firing without anything in the kiln, and you may have to make a note of the temperatures that correlate to numbers on the dial. Each kiln is unique; spend time getting to know it and you will be better able to use it successfully.

CLEAN IT OUT

If you've never used your kiln before, you'll need to prepare it for the first firing. It will probably be filled with dust or particles, which can get embedded in glass during firing. It's best to vacuum the interior thoroughly to be sure it's completely clean. Kilns are made of firebrick, a very soft material, so be careful not to damage it when vacuuming.

PROTECT THE KILN SURFACES

Both the kiln floor and the top surface of the kiln shelf will need to be protected so that your glass project doesn't stick to them and so stray bits of glass don't burn into the firebrick. This is accomplished by applying kiln wash or using fiber paper.

- **Fiber paper:** Using scissors, cut it to fit the shape of the kiln shelf, and then fire it to about 1200°F (650°C) to burn off the binder in the paper. Keep the kiln vent open, and make sure the room is well ventilated, as the paper releases an odor. Fiber paper can be reused, so be careful not to rip it when removing it. Always wear protective gloves and a particle mask when handling fiber paper because the fibers shouldn't be inhaled.

- **Kiln wash:** Mix this powder with water according to the manufacturer's directions. The use a paintbrush to apply at least four coats, brushing in a different direction each time. Let the kiln wash dry. When the coating begins to flake off, remove it completely with a paint scraper, vacuum the particles, and then reapply; be sure to wear a particle mask.

LOADING THE KILN

To properly heat glass, air needs to circulate around the piece. For this reason, glass is set on a kiln shelf, which is propped up with kiln posts. These accessories will most likely come with your kiln, along with guidelines for positioning them within your kiln. The kiln shelf needs to be protected with kiln wash or fiber paper as well.

KEEP A FIRING LOG

To repeat your successes and to avoid repeating mistakes, keep a firing log. Some of the things you should record are:

- The technique used: fusing, slumping, or other
- Type of glass used
- What happened to the glass at each temperature stage
- How long the kiln stayed at each temperature
- Whether you used fiber paper or kiln wash
- How often and how long you flash vented

As you gain experience, your firing log will likely become more sophisticated and detailed.

FUSING

There are many things for which your glass-working kiln can be used. Begin the creative journey by becoming familiar with the fusing process described here; then, explore the possibilities.

The process of fusing has five stages. The duration and temperature of each stage depends on the chosen glass, the kiln, and the kind of project you're making.

1. **Heating:** During this stage, glass is heated from room temperature to the fusing point.
2. **Soaking:** During this stage, the kiln is kept at a specific temperature for a period of time to allow the piece to continue to fuse or slump.
3. **Rapid Cooling:** During this stage, the kiln temperature is dropped to just above the annealing temperature range; this is accomplished by flash venting, which involves opening the kiln for a period of time.
4. **Annealing:** During this stage, the fused piece is cooled slowly and becomes solid again.
5. **Final Cooling:** During this stage, the glass has solidified and is allowed to slowly cool to room temperature.

KILNWORKING TERMINOLOGY

- **Fusing:** Pieces of glass are merged together to create a whole.
- **Slumping:** Molds are used to shape glass as it softens to create items such as bowls.
- **Combing:** Tools are used to manipulate the surface of softened glass.
- **Casting:** Small pieces of glass are fused inside a mold. See pages 106-107 for an example.
- **Pate de verre:** Glass "paste" is fused inside a mold.

THE HEATING STAGE

As a kiln reaches certain temperature ranges, the consistency and characteristics of your glass will go through discernable changes. Learning to understand and recognize these specific stages is the key to successful fusing.

Keep in mind that the temperature ranges listed below are approximate; the actual temperature at which a piece of glass reaches a certain stage will depend on the type, shape, and thickness of glass being used. This is one reason why it's important to understand the process and learn to recognize the stages rather than relying on temperatures as guidelines.

1. Room temperature to approximately 1000°F (540°C): Glass remains solid, but begins to expand.
2. 1000°F to 1300°F (540°C to 700°C): The glass begins to soften and look shiny.
3. 1300°F to 1400°F (700°C to 760°C): Glass pieces will begin to stick together; glass slumps fully.
4. 1400°F to 1500°F (760°C to 815°C): Slumped glass may begin to stretch out of shape. Two pieces of glass will become fully fused.
5. 1500°F to 1700°F (815°C to 927°C): Glass becomes molten and will begin to glow red. At around 1700°F (927°C), the glass can be combed. Attempt this only after you become comfortable with fusing and slumping.

SOAKING

Once the kiln reaches the desired temperature, the level of heat is maintained for a period of time before cooling the glass.

The amount of soaking time depends entirely on the effect you want to achieve. A longer soaking time during fusing will cause the glass to spread more, resulting in a smoother, flatter piece. A longer soaking time during slumping will also cause the glass to conform more closely to the mold. Check the progress of your piece and keep good records of the length of time needed to achieve particular effects. The kiln, type of glass, size, and thickness of the piece all have an effect on the soak time.

RAPID COOLING

Once your project has achieved the desired shape, it needs to be cooled quickly to stop any further fusing or slumping. This is achieved by flash venting, which simply involves holding the kiln open for several seconds. Be cautious when doing this, and wear protective gloves.

ANNEALING

Annealing refers to the slow cooling process, when glass gradually hardens. If glass is cooled too quickly, stress points and cracks will occur.

Different glass will anneal at different rates. When you begin, the safest way to cool a piece, especially when combining different glasses, is to do it as slowly as possible. This means minimizing the number of flash vents, keeping the kiln vents plugged, and making sure the room temperature is not too cold. The annealing stage begins when the natural color begins to return to the glass, and the kiln has cooled to approximately 1050°F (565°C).

FINAL COOLING

Once the piece is safely annealed, the final cooling stage begins, at about 750°F (400°C). Don't open the kiln or subject the room to temperature extremes at this point. This may cause the glass to crack.

Keep a record of the time it takes your kiln to cool. Larger pieces may require more time, and if your kiln naturally cools too quickly, try firing the kiln intermittently on a low setting to slow the cooling process.

FUSING STEP BY STEP

There are four major steps to creating a fused project: Cut the glass; load the kiln; fire the kiln; and clean and refine the piece.

1. Cut the glass. Review Cold Glass Basic Techniques on page 8, if necessary. The same techniques and tools apply to cutting glass for fused projects. Take care that the edges of the glass pieces are fairly smooth; any bumps and burrs will create a sloppy fused line. Wash and dry the glass using a lint-free cloth.
2. Load the kiln. Prepare the kiln and shelf using fiber paper or kiln wash. Layer your glass pieces on the kiln shelf; this can be done inside or outside the kiln. Place the shelf in the kiln.
3. Fire the kiln.
    a. Slowly raise the heat to the full fusing temperature indicated by the glass manufacturer.
    b. Soak the glass. Begin by following the guidelines provided by the glass manufacturer, and adjust as needed. Watch the glass carefully to monitor the progress. Refer to Fusing on page 61 if you need to adjust times and temperatures.
    c. Flash vent the kiln to just above 1050°F (565°C) by opening the kiln all the way for approximately eight seconds, and then close the door and check the temperature. Repeat the procedure until the temperature falls below 1100°F (595°C). Use extreme caution when doing this! The heat from the kiln will be intense. If your kiln doesn't automatically turn off when opened, turn it off manually (only while the kiln is open). This is a necessary safety precaution when using electric kilns
    d. Begin annealing the glass when the temperature drops to 1050°F (565°C). Control the rate of temperature decrease to about 3°F (-16°C) per minute. This is a very slow rate, which should work well for just about any glass. Remember—you can anneal too quickly, but not too slowly! To determine your kiln's rate of temperature increase and decrease for each setting, as well as the natural rate of cooling once the kiln is turned off, perform a test run and record the information in your firing log. This information is very helpful during the annealing process.
    e. Turn the kiln off and allow it to cool to room temperature once it reaches 750°F (400°C). Don't open the kiln during this stage.
4. Clean and refine the piece. Once the piece has cooled to room temperature, clean the piece. If you used fiber paper, gently peel it away while wearing gloves and a particle mask. Save it for later use, and then wash the glass. If you used kiln wash, you'll need to clean off any residue that stuck to the glass.

Try to keep the edges of your glass pieces as smooth as possible, like the ones seen here, if you want to maintain clean lines in the finished piece.

To smooth any rough edges, use a metal file, sandpaper, or an electric grinder (available from stained glass suppliers). To further refine rough edges, you may want to re-fire the piece to about 1200°F (650°C) to round the rough edges after filing or sanding them.

If your piece has unwanted bubbles or cracks, you've most likely fired the piece too quickly. Try slowing down different stages of the process, and keep records of how the glass reacts. This way, you'll discover exactly where the trouble lies and be able to consistently avoid it.

SLUMPING

Now that you understand the fusing process, try slumping—using a mold to shape glass. The firing process is the same as fusing, except that the optimum temperature for slumping is lower that the fusing point. The general range for slumping is about 1000°F to 1400°F (540°C to 760°C). So, if you want a slumped piece to have fused elements, you will need to do the fusing first. Then, refire the piece using a mold.

The actual temperature at which you reach the desired slumping effect will depend on the glass, kiln, and size of the piece. The slumping projects in this book call for Spectrum System 96™ glass; if you use it, you can follow the given temperature guidelines with confidence until you become more comfortable with the process.

SLUMPING OVER A MOLD

Slumping over stainless steel molds works best because steel contracts more than glass—which means it won't push into and interfere with the glass while it is slumping. Slumping over a mold creates beautiful draped folds.

SLUMPING INTO A MOLD

If you want to create a nicely round bowl or platter, allow the glass to slump into the mold. To prepare a mold for this technique, drill small holes in the bottom to allow the air to escape, or purchase a mold specifically designed for the task. Once you're ready to use the mold, cover the inside with several layers of kiln wash.

SELECTING A MOLD

Fusing suppliers offer commercial molds, but you can also make your own. Below are some of the materials that can be safely used as molds.

- **Stainless steel:** Lightweight, durable, and sturdy, stainless steel makes an ideal form. Simply coat it with a few layers of kiln wash. Try raiding kitchen supply stores for an inexpensive array of bowl molds. Because of the rate of expansion as compared to glass, it is best for slumping over.
- **Clay:** Slumping into pottery works well, once the surface is covered with a few layers of kiln wash. Because of the rate of expansion as compared to glass, it is best or slumping into.
- **Found items:** Tin cans, rocks, cement, and other items that can withstand the heat of the kiln can make interesting molds. Just coat with kiln wash, and test the piece in the kiln by slowly raising the heat (without any glass)to see how it behaves. This will also burn off any water or superficial residue that would interfere with slumping.
- **Ceramic fiber material:** Look for moldable ceramic fiber products from your kiln supplier. It can be shaped similar to the way papier-mâché is used.

FUSING
AND SLUMPING

In this chapter, you'll find projects to help you get acquainted with basic warm glass techniques. The first two projects, the Fern Plate on page 68 and the Organic Tiles on page 72, will guide you through the fusing process; the last two projects, the Art Glass Display Bowl on page 76 and the Fluted Candlestick on page 80, will introduce you to slumping techniques.

Once you become comfortable with the fusing process, you'll be amazed at the wonderful combinations of color and texture you can achieve by mixing and matching glass. Don't be afraid to experiment—it's the best way to learn and discover. Just be sure to follow the appropriate safety precautions.

If you've never fused glass or operated a kiln before, begin with a small fusing project before attempting a slumping project. To slump successfully, it's crucial to know your kiln and to be able to recognize the stages that glass goes through as it's heated. Don't worry—this won't take long!

Fern Plate

This project is a great way to learn how to illustrate using glass pieces. One of the most fascinating aspects of fusing is the way in which different glass merges to create interesting effects and colors. On this plate, a slight halo of darker green emerged around the fern elements, creating the illusion of depth. When designing a piece such as this one, keep in mind that glass spreads out a little when heated. This can be desirable or not—it depends on the look you're trying to achieve.

MATERIALS

• Basic fused glass tools and supplies (see page 58)

• 1 sheet of Spectrum System 96 fusing glass for the base, 12" x 12" (30 cm x 30 cm)

• ½ sheet of Spectrum System 96™ fusing glass for the fern design, 6" x 12" (15 cm x 30 cm)

DESIGNER'S TIP

Use a small dab of white glue to hold loose glass pieces in place when transporting a project to the kiln. Wait until the glue is tacky before positioning the pieces. Or simply layer the project in the kiln.

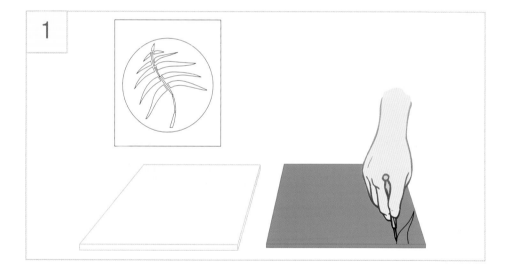

1. CUT, WASH, AND DRY THE GLASS PIECES. Photocopy and cut out the pattern pieces (see page 295). Score and break the glass as closely as possible to the edge of the pattern pieces; try to make the cuts as clean as possible. Groze the edges of the glass gently, if needed. Use a metal file or sandpaper to refine the edges of the pieces so that there aren't any outstanding bumps. Also try using a Dremel MiniMite fitted with a fine grinding tip for the smoothest finish.

Wash and dry the glass pieces, making sure they are free of lint or fingerprints.

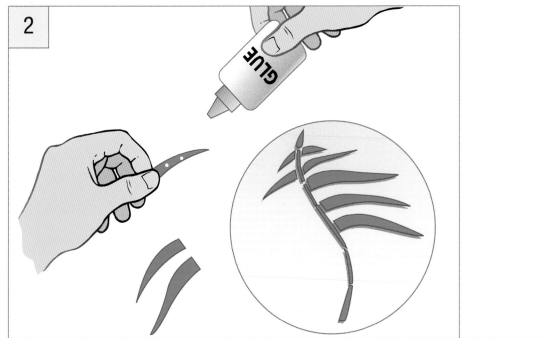

2. ARRANGE THE GLASS PIECES ACCORDING TO THE PATTERN. Layer the glass pieces as desired. Keep in mind that the pieces will spread about $\frac{1}{16}$" to $\frac{1}{8}$" (1.5 mm to 3 mm) when fused. To keep the elements of the design distinct, be sure to arrange the pieces at least $\frac{1}{16}$" to $\frac{1}{8}$" (1.5 mm to 3 mm) apart, or farther apart if you don't want the pieces to touch.

3. FUSE THE PIECE. Prepare and load the kiln as described on page 63. Turn the kiln on high with the vent open. Let it reach the manufacturer's specified fusing temperature for the glass. Carefully open the kiln and check the glass. If it is fused as desired, and then flash vent the kiln by opening the lid all the way for about eight seconds. If not, let the piece fire for a little longer, checking often.

After flash venting, turn off the kiln and plug the vents to soak the piece.

When the kiln temperature reaches 1000°F to 1100°F (540°C to 595°C), flash vent again, this time opening the lid only halfway for about four seconds. Let the kiln cool to room temperature for six to eight hours.

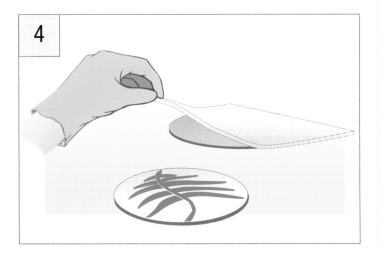

4. CLEAN AND FINISH THE PIECE. Clean the kiln paper or kiln wash residue off the piece. Then, file, sand, or use a Dremel MiniMite fitted with a fine grinding tip to smooth the edges.

TRADE SECRETS

Sometimes glass takes on a whitish, dull surface appearance with spots after being fired. This is one reason for the rapid cooling stage (see Fusing, page 61), which minimizes the amount of time spent in the devitrification temperature range of 1100°F to 1400°F (595°C to 760°C). You may or may not like the effect—some artists like the effect, whereas others try to avoid it.

To help prevent devitrification, use an overspray (or devit spray). Some sprays damage iridescent coatings on glass, so fire the piece with the iridescent side face down, and use the spray on the other side of the glass.

Complex designs can benefit from differences in the finish.

Organic Tiles

Layer flowers and foliage between two pieces of glass for striking, naturalistic designs. Here, we used fan-shaped gingko leaves of different sizes to make the white and green tiles and pink hydrangea blossoms to make the blue tile. The effect is an organic, fossil-like look. Experiment with different kinds of materials; each one will have a unique effect. However, you can count on the same material to produce the same look again and again.

MATERIALS

Makes 2 tiles:

- Basic fused glass tools and supplies (see page 58)

- ½ sheet of colored Spectrum System 96 fusing glass, 6" x 12" (15 cm x 30 cm)

- ½ sheet of clear fusing glass, 6" x 12" (15 cm x 30 cm)

- Dried and pressed leaves and flowers

DESIGNER'S TIP

Press your own flowers and leaves by placing them in the pages of an old telephone book. Lay more books on top to add more weight, if needed.

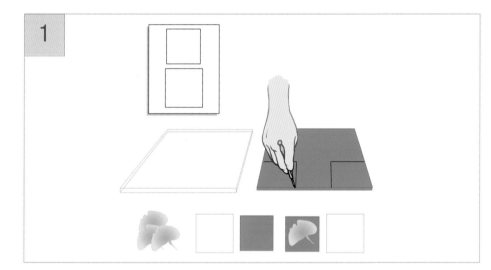

1. CUT, WASH, AND DRY THE GLASS PIECES. Photocopy and cut out the pattern pieces (see page 296). Score and break the glass as closely as possible to the edge of the pattern pieces; try to make the cuts as clean as possible. Groze the edges of the glass gently, if needed. Use a metal file or sandpaper to refine the edges of the pieces so that there aren't any outstanding bumps. Also try using a Dremel MiniMite fitted with a fine grinding tip for the smoothest finish.

Wash and dry the glass pieces, making sure they are free of lint or fingerprints.

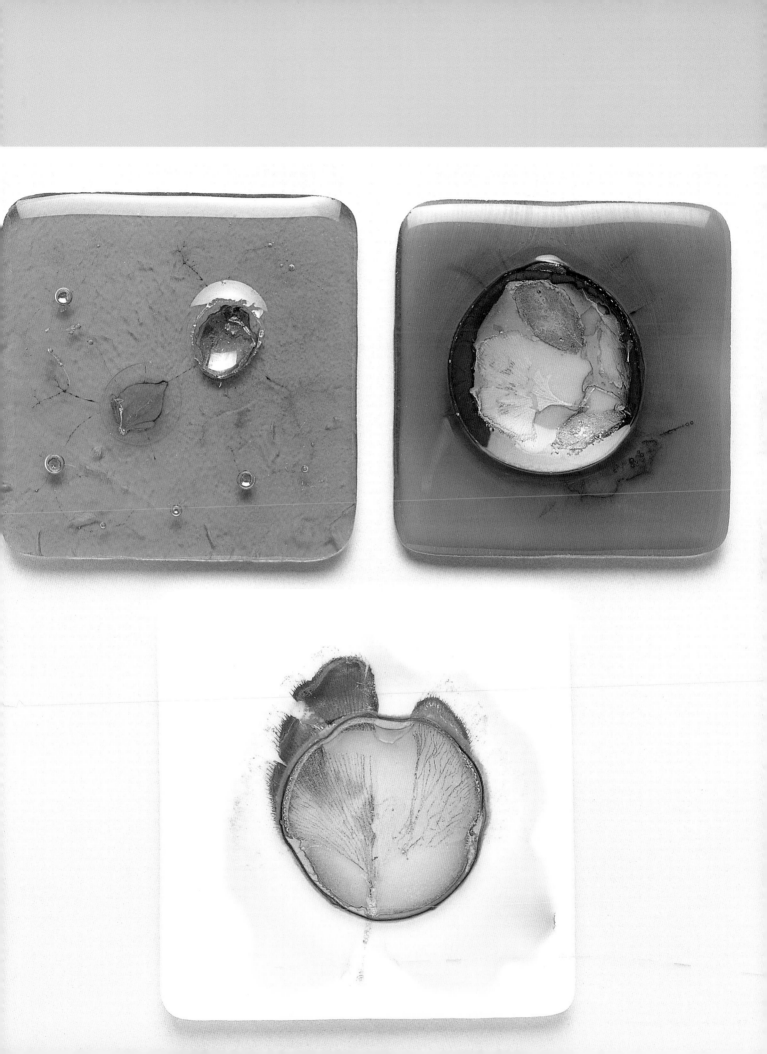

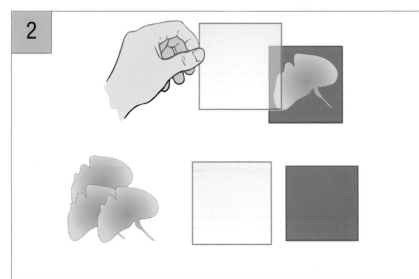

2. ARRANGE THE GLASS PIECES AND THE FOLIAGE AS DESIRED. Layer the foliage on top of the colored glass. Place the slightly larger clear glass on top. The overlap will slump and fuse to the bottom piece, creating smooth, rounded edges. Keep in mind that the embedded material will create a depression in the glass, which will be concentrated toward the center of the foliage.

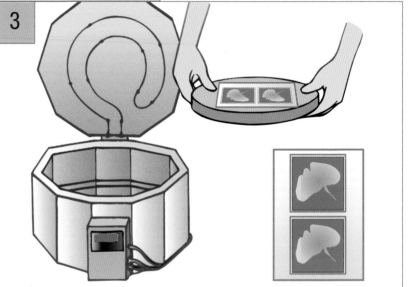

3. FUSE THE TILES. Prepare and load the kiln as described on page 63. Turn the kiln on high with the vent open. Calculate fifteen minutes per tile, and let the kiln fire for this amount of time. Then carefully open the kiln and check the tiles. The foliage should be ashen, and the glass should form a bubble over it. If it hasn't, let the tiles fire for a little longer, checking often. Then plug the vent. Let it reach about 50°F (10°C) above the manufacturer's specified fusing temperature for the glass.

Continue firing the tiles. After about twenty minutes, the temperature should be about 1700°F (926°C); the glass should be molten and glowing red. At this point, flash vent the kiln by opening the lid all the way for about eight seconds. Remove the plug from the vent.

Flash vent every twenty minutes until the kiln temperature reaches 1000°F (540°C), but open the lid only halfway for about four seconds. Let the kiln cool to room temperature for six to eight hours. After the kiln reaches 1000°F (540°C), do not open again until cooled to room temperature.

Kiln fiber paper leaves a textured imprint on glass, and the area will have a more matte finish. Many artists use this to their advantage by cutting shapes out of kiln paper and positioning them strategically on the surface of the project, or by sandwiching them between layers of glass.

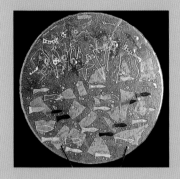

To create fish and seaweed shapes, the artist used cut pieces of kiln paper between two layers of glass, then fused the piece.

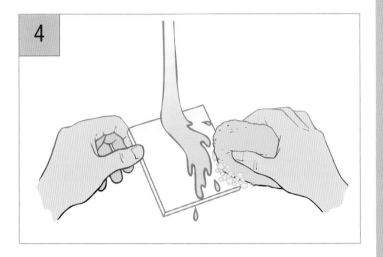

4. CLEAN AND FINISH THE PIECE. Clean the kiln paper or kiln wash residue off the piece. Then, file, sand, or use a Dremel MiniMite fitted with a fine grinding tip to smooth the edges.

Art Glass Display Bowl

This elegant bowl seems to glow with inner light. Luminous amber-colored glass complements the free-form shape, giving the piece a natural, earthy look. Make your own by simply laying a circle of glass over a mold, such as a humble stainless steel mixing bowl that may be hidden away in a cupboard. If the piece doesn't come out the way you'd like, try refiring it.

MATERIALS

- Basic fused glass tools and supplies (see page 58)

- One full sheet of Spectrum System 96 fusing glass, 12" x 12" (30 cm x 30 cm)

- Stainless steel mold (see Selecting a Mold, page 65)

DESIGNER'S TIP

Glass doesn't always slump the way you'd like. When this happens, use a metal skewer or similar tool to gently shape the flutes or drape of a project before cooling the piece.

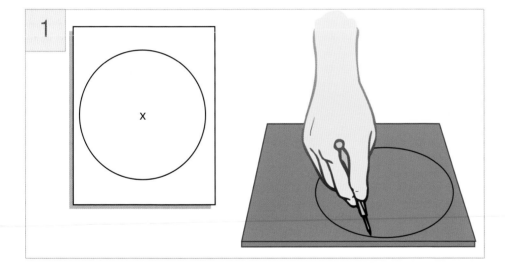

1. CUT, WASH, AND DRY THE GLASS. Photocopy and cut out the pattern (see page 297). Score and break the glass as closely as possible to the edge of the pattern pieces; try to make the cuts as clean as possible. Groze the edges of the glass gently, if needed. Use a metal file or sandpaper to refine the edges of the pieces so that there aren't any outstanding bumps. Also try using a Dremel MiniMite fitted with a fine grinding tip for the smoothest finish.

Wash and dry the glass pieces, making sure they are free of lint or fingerprints.

2. PREPARE THE MOLD. Find the center of the glass circle, and mark it by scratching the point with a knife or similar tool.

Prepare the mold by covering it with several layers of kiln wash (see also page 64). Lay the glass circle on the mold, making sure that the center point is aligned over the top of the mold.

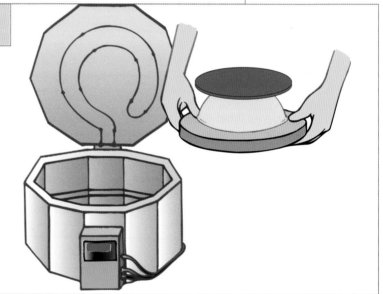

3. SLUMP THE GLASS. Prepare the kiln as described on page 63. Place the glass and mold in the center of the kiln. Turn the kiln on to a setting that corresponds to approximately 1250°F (677°C), with the vent open. When the temperature reaches 1000°F (540°C), carefully open the kiln and check the glass. It should begin to droop over the mold. When the kiln reaches 1100°F to 1150°F (595°C to 620°C), it will begin slumping.

Check often until the bowl reaches the desired look. When it does, turn off the kiln and flash vent by opening the lid all the way for about eight seconds. Put the plug halfway into the vent; you don't want to soak the piece after the desired amount of slumping is achieved. Let the kiln cool to room temperature for six to eight hours.

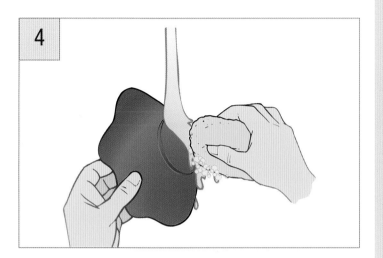

4. CLEAN AND FINISH THE PIECE. Clean the kiln paper or kiln wash residue off the piece. Then, file, sand, or use a Dremel MiniMite fitted with a fine grinding tip to smooth the edges.

TRADE SECRETS

As you gain experience in fusing and slumping, you'll begin to discover ways to guide the glass into doing want you want. This knowledge comes from observing the way glass behaves. For instance, the folds that occur in a slumped piece seem to be random—but you can control them to a great extent.

As a piece slumps, any heavier areas fall first. Take advantage of this by cutting or grozing scallops or other designs into perimeter of the glass circle; the areas where glass is taken away will tend to fall after the others. Alternatively, try adding fused decorations to certain areas of the circle. Then, when refiring it over or in a mold, these heavier fused areas will slump first.

Fluted Candlestick

This project involves carving your own mold from soft firebrick. Don't worry—it's much easier than it sounds (see Trade Secrets, page 83). The fabriclike folds created by slumping over a mold add to the graceful beauty of a lit taper candle. The amount of folding corresponds directly to the width of the mold. The wider the mold, the less dramatic the folds will be; the narrower the mold, the more pronounced the folds will be.

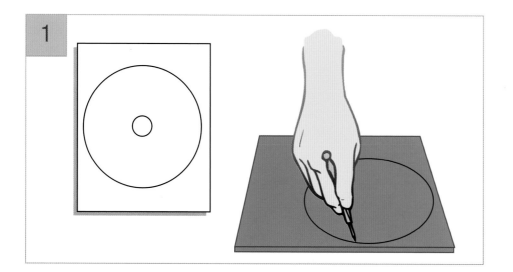

1. CUT, WASH, AND DRY THE GLASS. Photocopy and cut out the pattern (see page 298). Score and break the glass as closely as possible to the edge of the pattern pieces; try to make the cuts as clean as possible. Groze the edges of the glass gently, if needed. Use a metal file or sandpaper to refine the edges of the pieces so that there aren't any outstanding bumps. Also try using a Dremel MiniMite fitted with a fine grinding tip for the smoothest finish.

Wash and dry the glass pieces, making sure they are free of lint or fingerprints.

2. PREPARE THE MOLD. Find the center of the glass circle, and mark it by scratching the point with a knife or similar tool.

Prepare the mold by covering it with several layers of kiln wash (also see pages 64–65). Lay the glass circle on the mold, making sure that the center point is aligned over the top of the mold. To make the mold used for this project, see Trade Secrets, opposite.

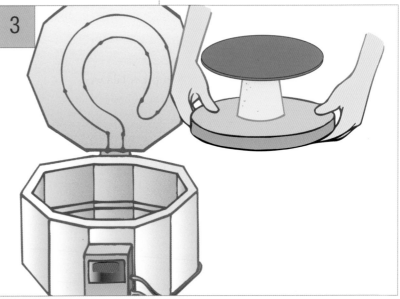

3. SLUMP THE GLASS. Prepare the kiln as described on page 63. Place the glass and mold in the center of the kiln. Turn the kiln on to a setting that corresponds to approximately 1250°F (677°F), with the vent open. When the temperature reaches 1000°F (540°C), carefully open the kiln and check the glass. It should begin to droop over the mold. When the kiln reaches 1100°F to 1150°F (595°C to 620°C), it will begin slumping.

Check often until the candlestick reaches the desired look. When it does, turn off the kiln and flash vent by opening the lid all the way for about eight seconds. Put the plug halfway into the vent; you don't want to soak the piece after the desired amount of slumping is achieved. Let the kiln cool to room temperature for six to eight hours.

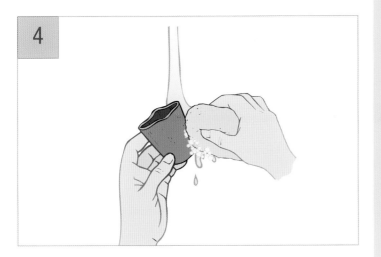

4. CLEAN AND FINISH THE PIECE. Clean the kiln paper or kiln wash residue off the piece. Then, file, sand, or use a Dremel MiniMite fitted with a fine grinding tip to smooth the edges.

TRADE SECRETS

Soft, lightweight firebrick makes a great mold for slumping because it is easily carved with an ordinary serrated knife. Imagine the possibilities—you are not limited to store-bought molds!

To carve a tapered mold to make the candlestick seen here, begin with a piece of firebrick about 2" x 4" (5 cm x 10 cm). Refine the shape using a knife and finally sandpaper. The finished dimensions should be about 1" (2.5 cm) at top, 1 ¹/₂" (4 cm) at the base, and about 3" (8 cm) high. This will make a mold suitable for the 7" (18 cm) circle of glass used in this project. To be sure that the finished piece is level on a table top, smooth and flatten the corresponding area on the mold until it rests.

Kilns are made of firebrick and come with firebrick accessories, so firebrick is readily available at any kiln supplier in various shapes and sizes.

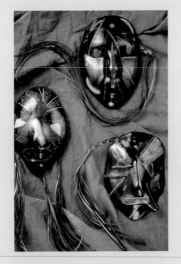

Try making your own mask molds using firebrick.

CONTINUING
THE JOURNEY

Now that you have learned the basics, let this gallery of artwork inspire you to expand your know-how. From traditional painting to kiln casting, the world of art glass is diverse and exciting. You'll get a taste of myriad styles of modern glass art—and a hint of what you can create yourself—from each of the talented artists whose work you will encounter on the following pages. Remember, you can go as far as you want; don't be intimidated by more advanced techniques. Everyone starts at the beginning.

To continue the journey, look to professional organizations, trade periodicals, and local suppliers for information on classes and communities of glass artists (see Resources, page 299). No matter how long you've been doing something, there's always something new to discover. Experienced artisans can learn as much from novices as novices can learn from them—a fresh perspective can be both invigorating and enlightening. This exchange is the lifeblood of art.

May your glass always break in an interesting (if unintentional) way!

Gallery of Art Glass

Giorgetta McRee, United States

Creating a picture with pieces of glass isn't only about color and shape. Glass often has embossed texture, like the sand seen here. The textured side is technically the back, but that doesn't mean you can't use it as the front!

Uriel. Sheets of glass have uneven, fluid-looking edges, which don't have to be trimmed away. One such edge inspired the face in this piece.

This holiday wreath is accented with glass drop jewels, which have a flat back. They are available in many colors and sizes and are an easy way to incorporate round, dimensional shapes into a stained glass piece.

Lamps are coveted stained glass pieces because of their elegance and grace. Kits, which include bases, frames, and wiring, are available from stained glass suppliers. In this lamp, opaque glass is used at the bottom and translucent glass is used at the top, which causes the light to diffuse upward.

Lit pieces don't always have to be lamp shades. The shell, which is translucent, makes a perfect focal point.

This lighted cube is a prime example of the intricate, mosaiclike detail that can be achieved with the copper-foil method. In traditional stained glass, these details would have to be painted.

The dragonfly components of these earrings and necklace are made of dichroic glass. The wings are clear glass, but the dichroic film on the surface makes them glisten and appear colored. The body is accordion glass, which has ridges that are reminiscent of a real dragonfly's body. The pieces are fused in one firing.

Like the dragonflies, these turtles are also made of dichroic glass. They are made by first fusing the patchwork accents to the turtle's back. Then, the head and legs are added in a second firing.

These pins are fused just enough to attach the glass pieces, so that the dimensional quality remains. Gold leaf accents fired on the surface of some are another way to add eye-catching details.

Photographer: Jim Padilla

These fused masks incorporate ribbon and some sandblasted details. The combination of textures, colors, and dimension create tactile, visceral designs.

This piece is appropriately entitled *Underwater Fantasy*. The scene was sandwiched between two layers of glass and then fired. The design consists of copper, brass, and gold leaf and dichroic glass. To create the ghost images, the artist cut kiln fiber paper into fish and seaweed shapes.

Photographer: Jim Padilla

This fused and slumped bowl features a lively, bold design. By layering the underside extensively with pieces of kiln fiber paper, the artist added textured impressions, which are created when the glass melts around the paper during fusing.

Photographer: Jim Padilla

The gorgeous beadwork on this sumptuous box accentuates the openwork pattern on the lid. The organic, detailed design comes almost entirely from the soldered elements.

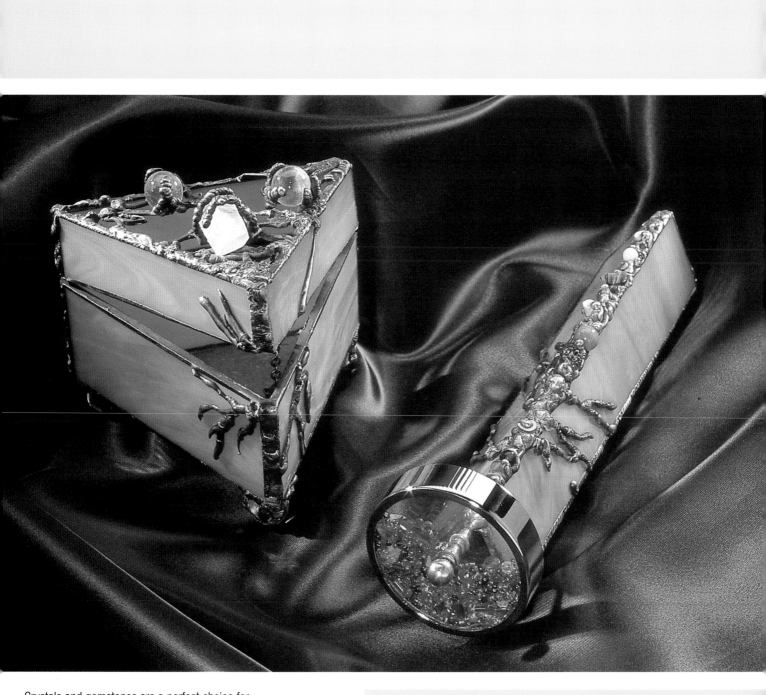

Crystals and gemstones are a perfect choice for adorning glass art because of their inherent luminosity, and often, translucency. The beads and gems on this box and kaleidoscope seem to grow naturally from the soldering.

Urban Man, 2000. The joyous figure seen at left was created using lacquer paint on 1/2" (1 cm) plate glass. The glass is sandblasted and has grozed edges.

Mambo, 2000. This couple was created entirely by sandblasting on 1/2" (1 cm) plate glass; the edges are grozed.

Shaman Mask, 1999. The untamed raffia accents on this brightly colored fused glass mask give it a primitive vigor. Combining glass with strikingly different materials can yield exciting, energetic pieces.

Arte en Vidrio, Mexico

Eng. Raul Urbina Torres, Mrs. Leticia Martínez de Urbina, and Mrs. Rosario Lopéz Balam

The artistic possibilities of fusing are readily apparent in this array of pendants. The pieces seen here have been fused with a variety of materials, including sand, silver, copper, and gold.

Fused tiles make striking architectural elements. Some of the ones shown above are not fully fused to retain some dimension. Imagine a mosaic made with custom tiles—the potential for illustrative work is exciting!

This Moroccan-style house in Mérida city is a breathtaking example of classic glass art. The artists of Arte en Vidrio who restored the beauty of the glasswork involved many techniques, including etching and high-fire painting.

The arched installation seen here is an example of traditional stained glass. The details are painted on large pieces of glass, creating a refined and classic work.

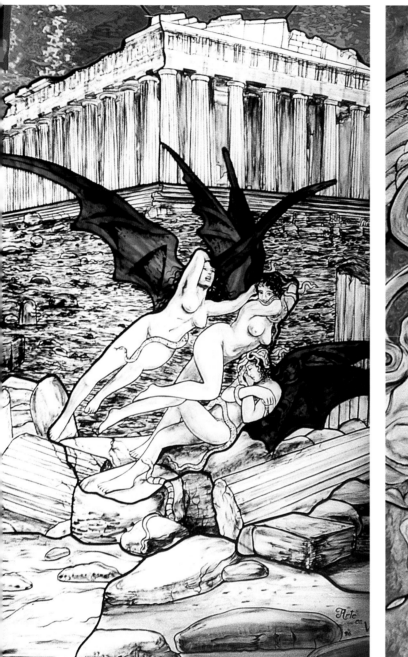 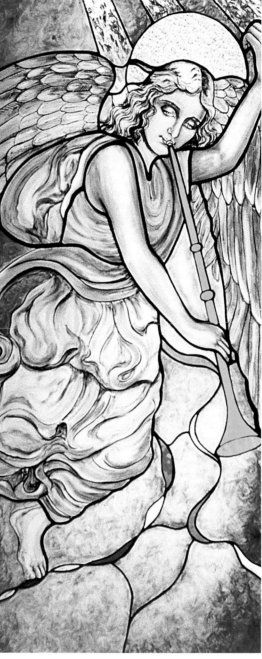

The two photographs shown above are more examples of traditional stained glass, as the details are painted. Notice the heavier dark lines, which indicate where the glass pieces are joined together. They follow the graceful curves of the design so as not to detract from the image.

Religion has inspired much of the world's greatest art. The window installations in this church are examples of innovative, modern glass art depicting the stations of crucifixion.

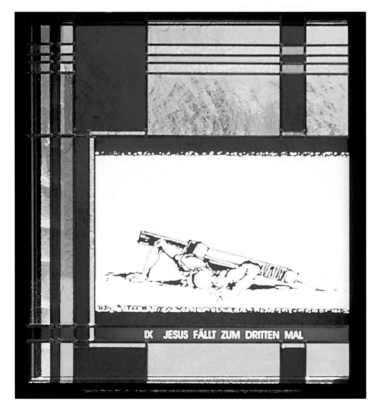

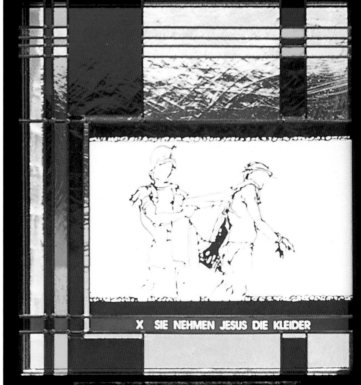

Detail: Jesus is being taken off the cross. The artist created these intricate illustrations by drawing them on antique blue glass using wood glue. Once the glue had dried, the rest of the glass was sandblasted to create the white space. Then, the glue was washed off, revealing the blue design.

Detail: Jesus is put to the grave.

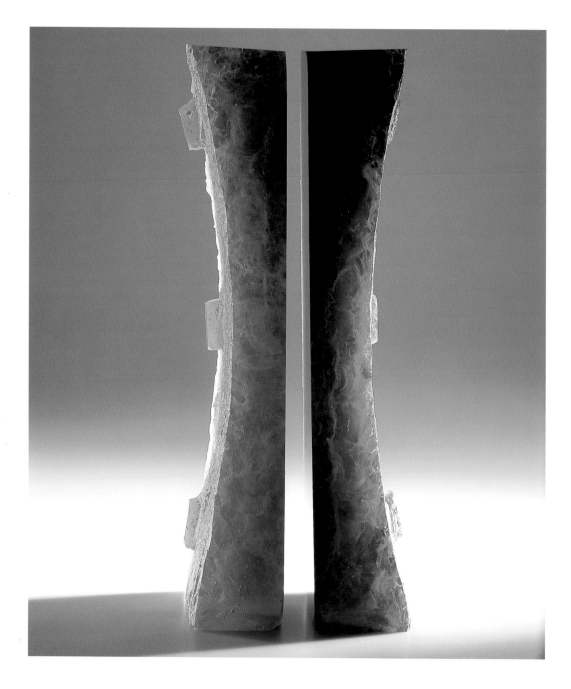

Paar. This sculpture was kiln cast, a technique that involves melting glass within a mold. Additional details were cut into the piece.

Stay. This sculpture involved a variety of techniques: casting, pouring molten glass, cutting, and sandblasting.

Anja Isphording, Canada

This vessels are made of kiln cast lead crystal, which was then cut and polished. The artist used the lost wax technique, which involves sculpting wax. This allowed her to create the fluid, curving details in the finished piece.

Glass, usually thought of as a rigid, cold material, can take on an amazing warmth and organic texture when sculpted in this manner—proving the amazing artistic versatility of glass and glass artists.

The vessels on both pages were both kiln cast using the lost wax technique. Both are reminiscent of delicate sea anemones, a look that surprises and delights when created with glass.

STAINED GLASS
POWERFUL COLORS

Stained glass is born from the fiery drama of an oven so hot it hurts just to look inside. The color and the drama become integral to the glass and cannot be erased. Glass artists through time have been drawn to the vivid colors and variations—mistakenly called "imperfections"—in the glass. Lit by direct or ambient light, stained glass panels have a life all their own, ripe with magnificent and seductive hues. Talented and visionary glass artists join pieces of this material in a process called *leading*, placing each piece in one side of a two-sided channel called *came*. The best artist acts as a composer, creating a symphony with the material and the lines that connect it.

Characteristic of the best stained glass artists, Rachel Schutt-Mesrahi takes this enigmatic material in new and challenging directions. Rather than ask, "Can it be done?" she inquires, "How will I do it?" Sigrídur Asgeirsdóttir also stretches the bounds of what many viewers traditionally consider glass art. As do all the artists featured in this book, she challenges her audience to think beyond the medium's obvious properties to glimpse statements that surpass the material.

David Wilson produces larger, more architecturally related statements. Using a muted palette that includes colorless glasses, he strives to improve buildings with the transmutation of natural light. Rick Melby, on the other hand, works with artificial light. His interior light fixtures combine a range of influences, from Bauhaus Germany to traditional Japan, in unique sculptural designs.

Lutz Haufschild also creates architectural art, striving to achieve an integrity that goes far beyond the medium. He aims to instill architecture with an essence and a spirit that elevate the entire structure. Kuni Kajiwara shares that goal as she approaches her commissions with one of two styles—precise geometry or simple abstract design.

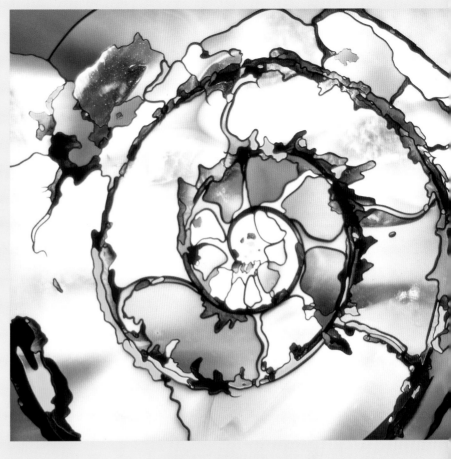

Rachel Schutt-Mesrahi
BACKLIT PANEL BEHIND ALTAR, JOHN MUIR HOSPITAL CHAPEL
(above and detail, opposite)
Life Unfolding
German blown glass, rondel pieces, copperfoiled and leaded
48" x 60" (122 cm x 152 cm)

Rachel Schutt-Mesrahi was first drawn to stained

glass by the material's ethereal qualities. She was

Rachel Schutt-Mesrahi

fascinated by the strong emotional response evoked

by the intensity of color and purity of light passing

through the glass. Beginning her career as a

craftsperson, Schutt-Mesrahi found herself intensely

inspired by the artistic process; thus, she made the

transition from craftsperson to stained glass artist.

Known for her eloquent execution, the artist

bases her pieces on subjects from uniquely personal

sources. Even though she has long admired the work

of artists such as Clifford Stills and Marcel Duchamp,

she relies on an internal muse. Schutt-Mesrahi puts

great faith in the universality of the experiences she

shares through her art. Personal and transgenerational

WINDOW IN PRIVATE COLLECTION
Static Movement
German blown glass, leaded and copperfoiled
30" x 70" (76 cm x 178 cm)

INDEPENDENT PANEL
Emerging Self (Self Portrait)
German blown glass, leaded and copperfoiled, copper foil overlays
36" x 24" (91 cm x 61 cm)

loss, the emotional balance between being an artist and being a mother, and the stories we all share in different ways serve as the subjects of, and inspiration for, her work.

More than anything else, though, Schutt-Mesrahi's work focuses on how we hide experiences and, more importantly, how we slowly reveal them to ourselves and each other. Thus, the cracks in her sidewalks crumble to reveal a new and different perspective behind. Dark colors melt into lighter hues, shading defines clarity, and a tentative balance between the obscured and the apparent are everywhere in Schutt-Mesrahi's creations.

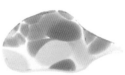

technique

Rachel Schutt-Mesrahi

When I start a design, I never think about the limitations of glass. What's important to me is that I convey the image that I want. When the image is drawn, I determine if the sheets of glass are big enough to use, if I can get the transitions I want with the shapes I've drawn, and if I need more lines to convey

more transitions. When I go to my table to work, I want to feel the same excitement I feel when I design, so I push the material.

In seeking to test the limits, I often develop interesting techniques. A good example is the issue of line work. I want to run lead lines where they normally would not go. I manage to do this by cutting the heart out of the lead channel to run it right over a section of glass on either side of the panel.

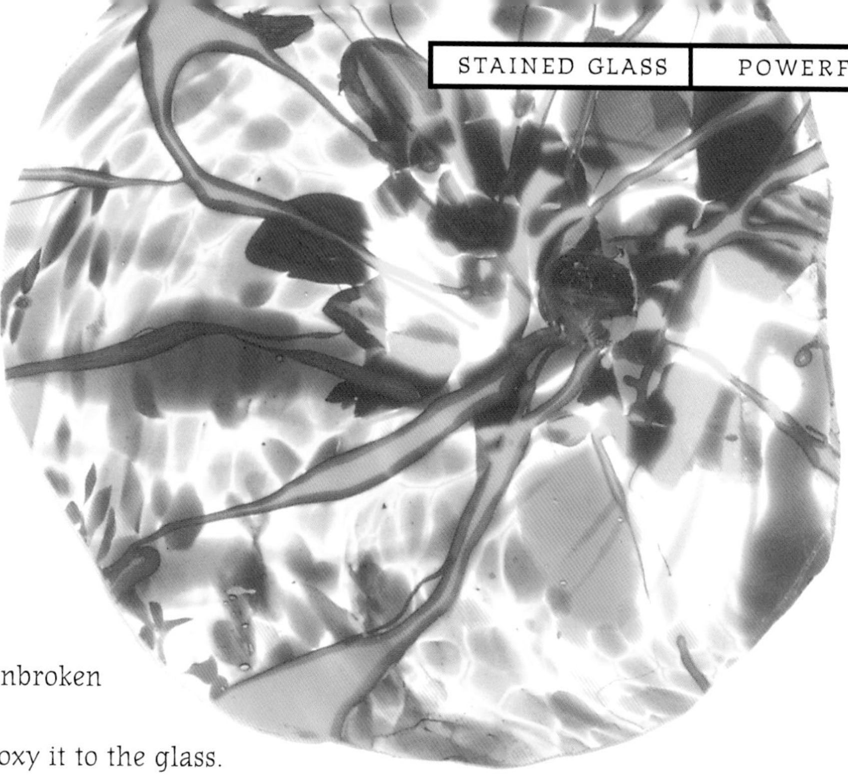

The lead floats on the unbroken

surface and I lightly epoxy it to the glass.

Using this

method,

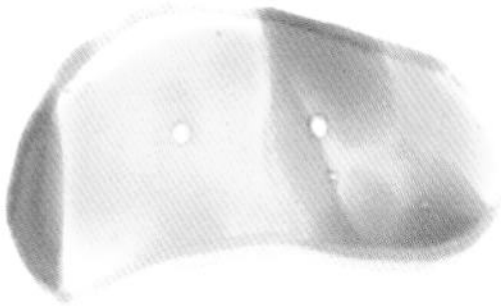

I can put a line almost anywhere

in the design.

When I am constructing my pieces, I feel like I am building something. I started out as a craftsperson because I loved working with my hands and the way the materials responded when I worked with them. After all these years, I still find myself as excited and challenged with this material as I was when I first started. I've never lost the love of working with leaded stained glass.

INDEPENDENT PANEL
Autumn Upheaval
German blown glass, etched
glass, leaded and copperfoiled
49" x 30" (124 cm x 76 cm)

INDEPENDENT PANEL
Circuitous Shadows
German blown glass, glass jewels, leaded,
copperfoiled with sheet lead overlays
3' x 3' (.9 m x .9 m)

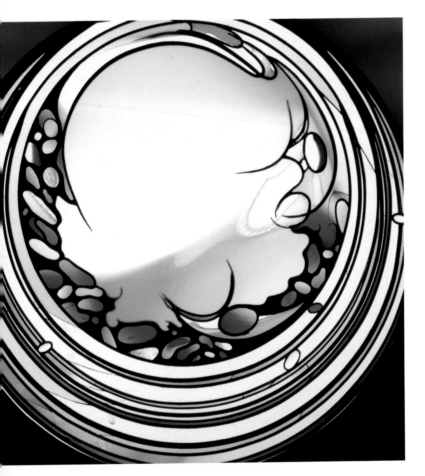

Rachel Schutt-Mesrahi

INDEPENDENT PANEL
Basking in the Glory
German blown glass, leaded
with sheet lead overlays
38" x 34" (97 cm x 86 cm)

WINDOW
Shadows Moving
German blown glass, glass jewels, leaded
21" x 55" (53 cm x 140 cm)

DOUBLE DOORS
Movement Through Ethos
German and Fremont blown glasses, rondels
66" x 21" (168 cm x 53 cm)

David Wilson's charismatic commissions could easily stand alone as stunning works in glass. But viewing his art in isolation

David Wilson

would defy the artist's greater purpose of establishing a partnership with the building and with its designer. Through his creations, Wilson gives due consideration to the sometimes unspoken exchange of ideas among the architect, those who use the space, and the artist. His constant awareness of the structural limitations of a particular space and the desires of his client serve to temper his considerable artistic skill.

Wilson's sensitivity to subject and user seems almost innate. His creative abilities, however, are the result of five years of rigorous fine-arts college education in his native England, culminating in postgraduate work at the Central School of Arts and Crafts in London. There, he studied stained glass, mural painting, and sculpture. He would later spend more than a decade as a craftsman and designer for a prominent stained glass studio in New York City.

Leaving the studio environment behind, Wilson expanded on the geometric forms that had earlier captured his imagination. Geometry remains the starting point for his design process. He creates a linear image, adding color and form to that foundation. In a process he terms "reductionist," Wilson develops only the elements that seem fundamental to the nature of the piece. This stripping away of superfluous elements creates a more essential and powerful design that does not suffer from the artist's subtle use—or complete dismissal—of color.

WINDOW, KENAN FLAGLER SCHOOL OF BUSINESS (detail)

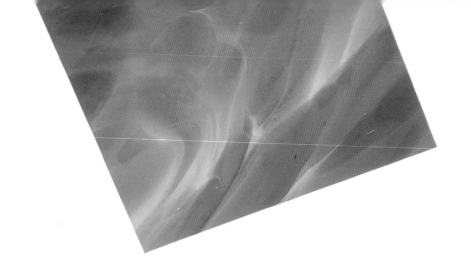

The first technical or visual aspect I consider is light. Light illuminating stained glass art—with the exception of artificially illuminated windows—is constantly changing. This is true not only through the day but also with the seasons.

The graphic quality of the lead line is yet another challenge. I find the lead line constantly intriguing.

Leaded glass has been incorporated in cathedrals in Europe since the Middle Ages, so you know that the technique works. Most of the work I have done is crafted in this traditional process, less often using brass, copper, or zinc channels as alternatives to lead. This does impose a certain aesthetic limitation, but it's a technical process with which I know I'm not going to have problems.

However, some architects find lead lines too busy. Consequently, one of the techniques I have been pursuing is treating

technique

David Wilson

larger sheets of structural glass with processes

other than the traditional ones. When you can

use sandblasting or special painted treatments on

larger surfaces, it opens up a new dimension in

the treatment of large, unbroken areas of glass.

Given the demands of my work and my

desire for large, unified planes, I am also investi-

gating sandwiching pieces of colored glass between

layers of structural glass without adhesives.

Ultimately, I want my work to incorporate

traditional and new techniques to take the union

of building and glass art one step further.

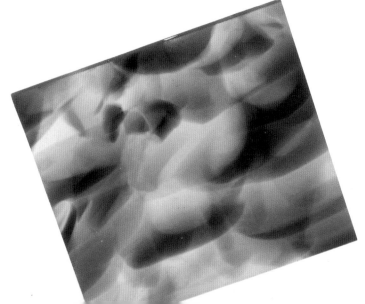

BARREL VAULT WINDOW,
ST. PAUL'S CATHOLIC CHURCH
Mouthblown transparent colors,
opalescents, and solar-tinted
window glass
20' x 16' (6.1 m x 4.9 m)

David Wilson

DOORS
Mouthblown transparent colors, opalescents,
dichroic glass, "spotted" glass, and clear bevels
7' x 18' (2.1 m x 5.5 m)

WINDOW
Mouthblown transparent colors, opalescents,
"spotted" colors, clear bevels
3' x 3' (.9 m x .9 m)

NEW JERUSALEM WINDOW,
CHRIST THE KING CATHOLIC CHURCH
Mouthblown antique transparent
colors, opalescents, and gold mirror
12' x 10' (3.7 m x 3 m)

WINDOW
Mouthblown antique transparent colors,
opalescents, and dichroic glass, copper channel
4' x 6' (1.2 m x 1.8 m)

Rick Melby's glass art light fixtures serve both as a testament to his talent and as a statement on

the amazing versatility of the medium. Melby worked in a traditional glass studio for only a few years before striking out on his own to create work that trades the changing nuances of sunlight for those of a constant, artificial light source. In his light fixtures, Melby establishes an interplay between dynamic color and a sense of movement.

Melby's designs reflect varied influences, ranging from the line work of the art nouveau and art deco movements to the simple expression of seventeenth-century Japanese art. But one of the strongest influences on his artistic development was more thematic than stylistic. Melby found in the work of Marcel Duchamp a talent for presenting the mundane and everyday as new and interesting, an inclination that informs many of Melby's own pieces.

Like much of Duchamp's work, Melby's art is an exploration of context, of juxtaposing materials and concept in novel and thought-provoking ways. Melby focuses as much on how the art will be seen and perceived as on how it is executed. He hopes to lead the viewer to look beyond the obvious, to see how objects can be relevant on several levels, not all of which are connected to the work's original intent.

WALL SCONCE (opposite)
Cloud Light
Custom-made hand-cast opalescent glass,
etched glass fins, glass rod, copperfoiled
10" high x 12" wide x 5" deep (25 cm x 30 cm x 13 cm)

technique

Rick Melby

Much of my work utilizes techniques I learned in working with leaded glass. I simply applied these processes to three-dimensional forms. Over the years, I have picked up other techniques, including glass blowing, etching, and fusing.

I want my work to hold together over time, which is a challenge with light fixtures because of the heat problem. Even a modest bulb can generate a lot of heat, causing the copper foil that holds a piece together to come apart, or making the lamp too hot to touch, or even cracking the glass.

Consequently, I have to design a way for the heat to escape, but I also have to keep in mind the positioning of the light source. If I use a large piece of clear or fairly translucent colored glass, the bulb may create a visual hot spot that detracts from the design. Although I sometimes use this hot spot as a design element itself, I usually want to eliminate it. After I've designed and built the piece, I test it in my studio for quite some time before delivering or installing it.

Of course, safety is the ultimate concern in building and installing my work. I am very careful because a badly wired lamp can cost people their belongings, their home, and more. The challenge is to create an artwork that safely adds to the aesthetics of the environment and serves the utilitarian purpose of providing light.

TABLE-TOP LAMP
Las Olas
Hand-cast opalescent and machine-rolled glasses,
copperfoiled and leaded, painted wood base
14" high x 17" long x 4" wide (36 cm x 43 cm x 10 cm)

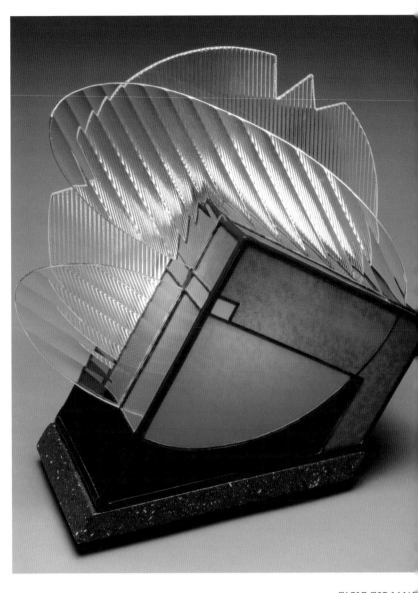

Rick Melby

TABLE-TOP LAMP
Orbr
Hand-cast opalescent and machine-rolled glasses
copperfoiled and leaded, painted wood base
13" high x 13" long x 5" wide (33 cm x 33 cm x 13 cm

TABLE-TOP LAMP
Untitled
Opalescent and machine-rolled glasses,
copperfoiled and leaded, painted wood base
17" high x 12" long x 4" wide
(43 cm x 30 cm x 10 cm)

TABLE-TOP LAMP
Wing Thing
Hand-cast opalescent and etched machine-rolled
glasses, copperfoiled and leaded, painted wood base
12" high x 17" long x 4" wide (30 cm x 43 cm x 10 cm)

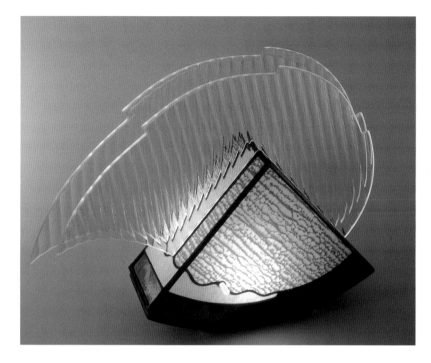

TABLE-TOP LAMP
Stratus
Hand-cast opalescent and etched machine-rolled glasses,
copperfoiled and leaded, painted wood base
13" high x 16" long x 5" wide (33 cm x 41 cm x 13 cm)

SCULPTURE
Scream
Etched plate glass, gold leaf, painted wood base
18" high x 11" long x 4" wide (46 cm x 28 cm x 10 cm)

Lutz Haufschild strives to reveal a building's soul with his architectural glass art. To him,

Lutz Haufschild

glass art has a lofty purpose and must endow the light entering the building with a significance that ultimately influences how the entire structure is perceived. He has pursued this goal for almost three decades, in small and large projects.

To create architectural art that meets these goals, Haufschild thinks beyond the material to the potential of the commission. He chose glass as a medium not because he fell in love with it, but because it allows him to work on an architectural scale that would be impossible in almost any other art form.

Haufschild does, however, consider in detail how an idea will translate into its material form. A project must expand his range and present new challenges that call for thoughtful solutions. The answer may lie in painting and etching a simple, vibrant design, such as *Blue Heart*, or in laminating bevels on plate glass, as with *Spectra Veil Sample*. His goal always remains the same: to continue a meaningful architectural artistic language that has a positive effect on the people who experience it.

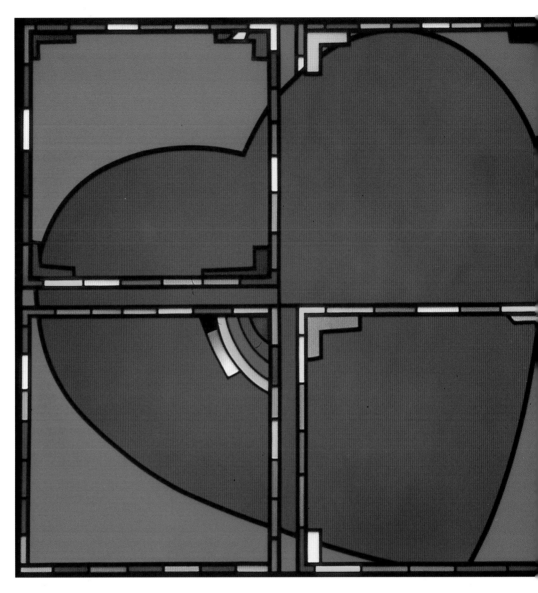

WINDOW
Blue Heart
Etched and painted glasses
30" x 30" (76 cm x 76 cm)

INTERIOR GLASS WALL (opposite)
Spectra Veil Sample
layers of etched glass and painted
antique glasses, laminated
30" x 48" (76 cm x 122 cm)

technique
Lutz Haufschild

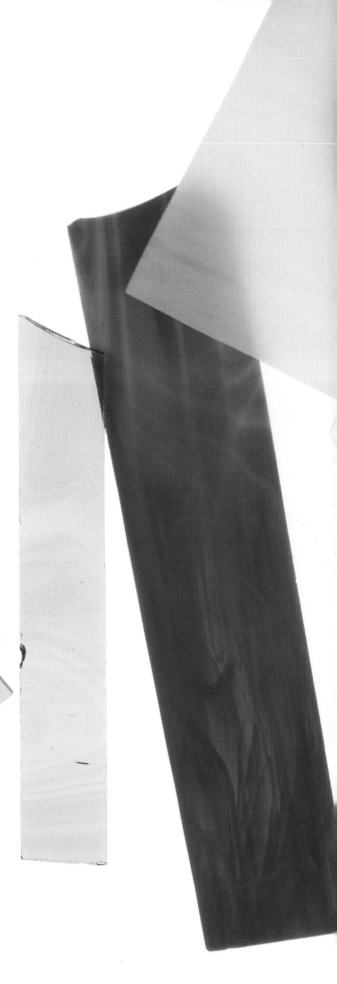

The desire to learn and to express myself in new ways has led me to experiment with new techniques and materials. For example, in trying to overcome the limitations of the lead line, I began to experiment with different laminating processes. In the commission *The Spectra Veil* for Toronto's Bata Shoe Museum, three layers of bevels and antique glass were laminated onto two layers of float glass. Although I used only clear glasses, by placing them in front of each other, an unusual opacity is achieved that fulfills the architectural requirements.

Because of this arrangement, the glass wall provides a new experience of the light itself.

I often work in large architectural formats. The complexity and size of my projects make it impossible to execute them myself. Since 1981 I have collaborated with three studios to fabricate my designs: Kits Glass Studios in Vancouver, Canada; Wilhelm Derix Glass Studios in Taunustein and Franz Meyer Studios in Munich, both in Germany. I work closely with the studios to ensure that my projects are completed true to the intent of the design, but I give them a lot of leeway because I like to benefit from their superior technical knowledge and experience.

Lutz Haufschild

BACKLIT INSTALLATION FOR STADIUM ENTRANCE
(detail showing Pete Rose)
Tribute to Baseball
Cast glass, total piece
60' x 16' (18.3 m x 4.9 m)

WINDOW IN CIVIC CENTER
The Fire Fighting Window
Layers of etched and painted antique glasses, laminated
8.5' x 16' (2.6 m x 4.9 m)

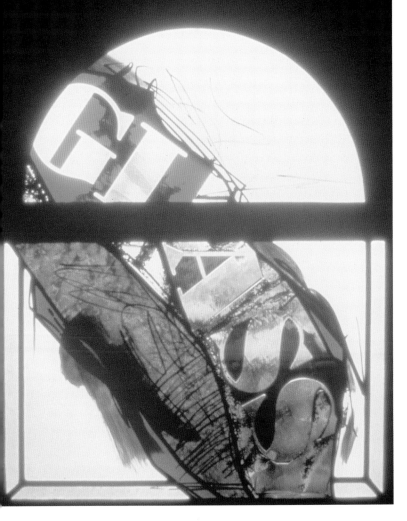

WINDOW, MUSEUM OF CONTEMPORARY GLASS
Gl/ass
Etched and painted stained glasses
48" x 36" (122 cm x 91 cm)

INTERIOR GLASS WALL, CORPORATE HEADQUARTERS
Time and Space
Etched and painted glasses
8.5' x 8' (2.6 m x 2.4 m)

ONE OF FOUR CHURCH WINDOWS (WINTER)
The Four Seasons
Etched and painted antique glasses
32' x 6' (9.8 m x 1.8 m)

Kuni Kajiwara first became fascinated with the potential of stained glass as an art student in Kobe, Japan. Her

Kuni Kajiwara

initial interest was heightened during her studies of graphic design in London. To Kajiwara, the stained glass windows in many of the older European buildings seemed almost three-dimensional in their vibrancy. She was transfixed by the metamorphosis of light into color and decided to pursue her own vision in this brilliant art form.

From the start, Kajiwara's exploration has gone in two design directions. In one aspect of her work, she creates a contemporary look, using a detailed and elaborate geometric vocabulary with subtle complementary colors. This work—exemplified by the skylight she created for the Hotel Taishoya—is precise, clean, and balanced.

In contrast, Kajiwara also crafts richly colored abstract pieces. She often works with *dalle de verre*, known as slab glass, to create dense, primitive pieces that reflect more pure emotion than exacting glass cuts. This work reflects the gentle, understated nature of an older Japan, the Japan of calligraphy, Shinto temples, and Zen gardens.

The two sides of Kajiwara's style find equal voice in her commissions. She doesn't feel she has to choose between the two, because each has different strengths and only one will be appropriate in a given space. The result is an ideal match of artwork to space.

SKYLIGHT, HOTEL TAISHOYA
Untitled
Handblown stained glass, painted glass
16.4' x 16.6' (5 m x 5.1 m)

I live in a remote area of Japan that is very beautiful and informs most of my design efforts, even when they are geometric in style. I can sit and look out over rice fields and mountains, which give me a lot of inspiration for sketching. I find sketching is a great exercise and really frees my creativity before I have to take on the technical considerations inherent in fabricating my pieces. All of my lines and colors come from the sketchbook first and foremost.

The commission I am working on usually determines my design style that, in turn, determines what the technical considerations will be. My geometric compositions may be more complex than my abstract designs, but they are usually easier to design because the linear nature of the piece makes it easier to include structural reinforcement. I find that geometric designs work better for large or difficult installations, such as skylights.

technique

Kuni Kajiwara

When working with abstract designs, I often like to work with *dalle de verre. Dalle de verre* comes in foot-long slabs that I cut with a chisel to create the pieces for my design. The beauty of this glass is that it is more than an inch thick, which makes the color very saturated, very dark and dramatic. My two different styles offer different technical and aesthetic challenges and, using both, they always seem fresh to me.

WINDOW, SAISEIKAI HOSPITAL
The Life
Dalle de verre, in epoxy and sand frame
7' x 8' x 4" (2.1 m x 2.4 m x 10 cm)

WINDOW
Banksia
Stained glass, etched and painted, with appliqué
28" (71 cm) in diameter

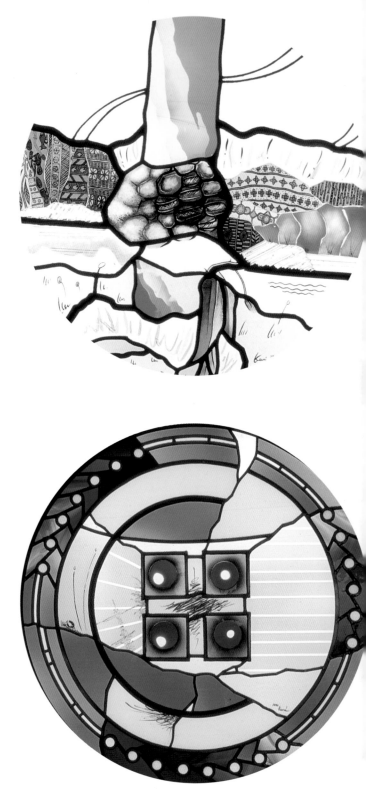

Kuni Kajiwara

WINDOW
Parnassius
Laminated stained glass, painted and sandblasted
30" (76 cm) in diameter

SKYLIGHT
Mandrara
Laminated stained glass, etched, painted, and sandblasted
6' x 4" x 8' (1.8 m x 10 cm x 2.4 m)

WINDOW, FUJI CITY LIBRARY
Untitled
Dalle de verre
12' x 3' x 3" (3.7 m x .9 m x 8 cm)

Sigrídur Asgeirsdóttir breaks the rules. This innovative Icelandic glass artist challenges the

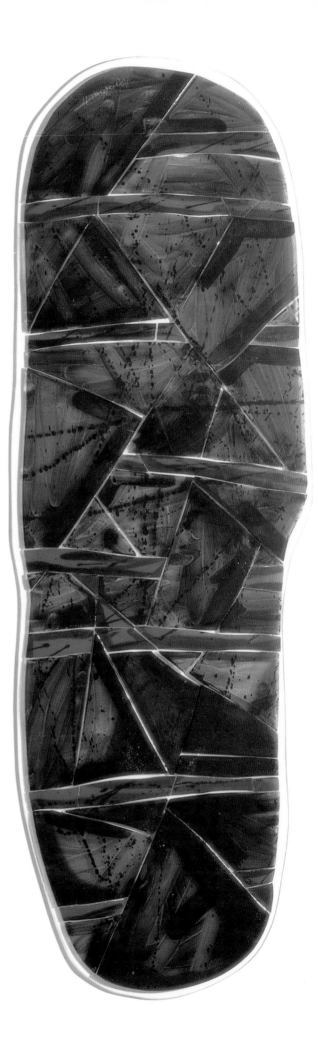

Sigrídur Asgeirsdóttir

very convention that, on the face of things, makes glass art distinctive: its transparency. She uses dense glass colors and dark reflective paints to focus interest on the design, the positioning of the pieces, and the play of shadows and light on edges and surfaces.

Asgeirsdóttir has long created intense designs in glass. Her recent exhibition pieces undermine all assumptions viewers may have about glass. In panels alive with one or two energetic colors, she crafts a language of hard-edged angles and violent splashes of glass paint. Using repetitive

EXHIBITION PIECE
Genesis
Laminated stained glass on clear glass, thick painting
59" x 23.5" (150 cm x 60 cm)

and juxtaposed panels, Asgeirsdóttir establishes an entirely different way of viewing the material.

Art critics and peers have commented that this drama of contrasts and forceful presentation echoes the harshness and beauty of Asgeirsdóttir's homeland. But this interpretation discounts the originality of her inspiration and creativity. She was first drawn to glass because of its contradictions—the tension in the material between its fragility and its forcefulness—and its power to transform. Asgeirsdóttir has taken that fascination a giant leap forward to a place where the viewer must leave preconceived ideas at the door and expect only the unexpected.

WINDOW
Gardar & Nattfari
Stained and clear textured glasses
29.5' x 29.5' (9 m x 9 m)

technique

Sigrídur Asgeirsdóttir

Because I was taught well, technical and structural demands are always in the back of my mind. But I do play with them in my sculptural works.

I often float very big pieces on a wall without any visible means of support, or I may lean a piece against a wall looking slightly out of balance. I think this generally goes unnoticed by nonexpert viewers, but those familiar with the weight of glass will be pleasantly surprised.

Technically, these pieces are great fun to create. The heavy glass base has to be cut and drilled by an outside vendor, while at the studio we are cutting the image, cleaning it, and lining it up for the paint. When the glass is ready to be

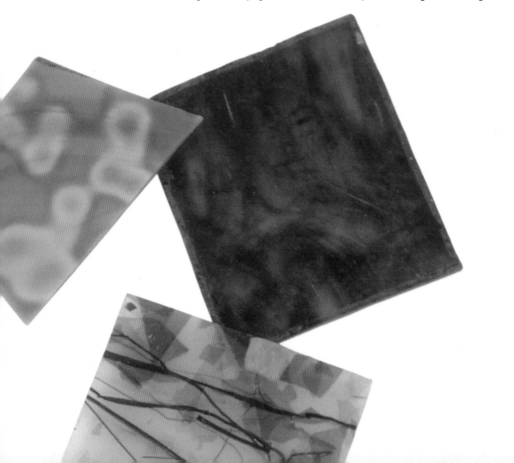

painted, the studio goes quiet and the air is filled with tension. Painting on glass for me is a very physical thing—the smell, the loading of the brush, the immediate impact of the paint to the glass. It is like a never-ending love affair. I still cut glass when I have to, but I rather think of myself as a conductor making sure that the emotion and thought get transferred from the sketch to the finished piece. I have no need to be all the instruments, only to know that they are working together.

Sigrídur Asgeirsdóttir

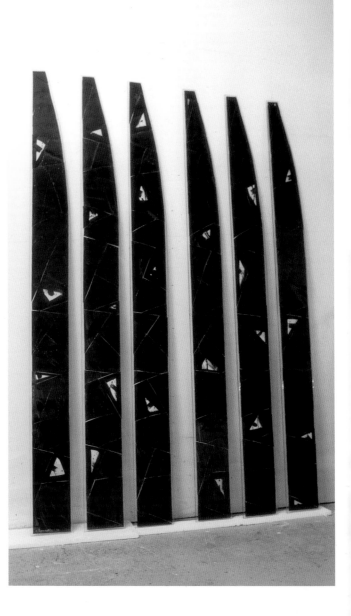

EXHIBITION PIECE
Triangles
Stained glass, painted and laminated on clear glass
39.5" x 98.5" (100 cm x 250 cm)

EXHIBITION PIECE
The Silence of the Sea
Stained glass, painted and laminated on clear glass
59" x 71" (150 cm x 180 cm)

INDEPENDENTLY HUNG PANEL
Untitled
Stained and clear glasses, painted
19.5" x 19.5" (50 cm x 50 cm)

INTERIOR WINDOW,
CORPORATE BUILDING
Night
Stained glass
39.5' x 9.75' (12 m x 3 m)

BEVELED GLASS
MAGNIFICENT ANGLES

Kenneth vonRoenn
GLASS COLUMNS
UNIVERSITY OF TOLEDO
(detail, above)

It has been said that diamonds fall second to the crisp, linear brilliance and charismatic glitter of beveled glass. An exaggeration, perhaps, but not by much. Beveled clear glass acts as a prism, splitting transmitted light into a transient rainbow of sparkling hues. Because of this property, the technique continues to gain popularity among contemporary glass artists.

Larry Zgoda uses custom-beveled jewels as thematic threads running through his timeless architectural panels. His designs complement the spaces they occupy, adding vivid focal points without overpowering other elements of the architecture. Shelley Jurs prefers to exploit negative and positive spaces within her panels, creating works that rely more on eloquence of lines and opposing forms than on the impact of strong colors.

Virginia Hoffman plays with the perception of bevels as fairly orderly pieces of glass. She creates fluid, abstract glass art, designing the bevels in odd, irregular shapes that bend and curve to the needs of the design. In contrast, the talented architectural stained glass artist Kenneth vonRoenn has increasingly worked with straight-line rectangular bevels. His linear designs offer textural interest that intensifies the innate sensual appeal and tactile allure of the glass.

Finally, Carl Powell uses innovative beveling techniques to bring his panels to life. He bevels both sides of the glass and uses other tricks of the trade to create designs full of active optical and geometric illusions.

Kenneth vonRoenn
WINDOW
Untitled
Beveled squares and rectangles, stained glass
2' x 4.9' (.6 m x 1.5 m)

Larry Zgoda's appreciation of stained glass as an architectural art form began almost three

Larry Zgoda

decades ago, when he spent much of his free time

photographing prewar buildings in Chicago. He developed an admiration for the elegant ornamentation—especially the stained glass— that was so much a part of the charm of those older buildings.

His fascination led him to a basic course in stained glass. He quickly expanded on this foundation, learning from other craftsmen, books, and trial and error. Taking a job with a dealer of architectural ornamentation, Zgoda spent two years rebuilding vintage stained glass panels and re-creating old styles in new panels. He eventually opened his own studio and began developing his own unique style in glass.

INTERIOR WINDOW BETWEEN TWO ROOMS
Beveled ruby jewels, black and red stained glasses,
beveled machined glass
16" x 34" (41 cm x 86 cm)

Zgoda's art focuses on the relationship of the glass design to its architectural context. To this end, he uses color sparingly, allowing large sections of clear glass to act as a foil for smaller pieces of subdued color. This sensitive balancing of color and light results in panels that complement the architecture. Unusual beveled pieces attract the viewer's eye and entice further exploration of architectural forms and colors.

The essence of Zgoda's talent lies in his ability to cut away clutter and still maintain enough complexity and interaction of geometric form to create intense visual interest. He uses this ability in pursuit of his ongoing goal to help revive the lost spirit of architectural art.

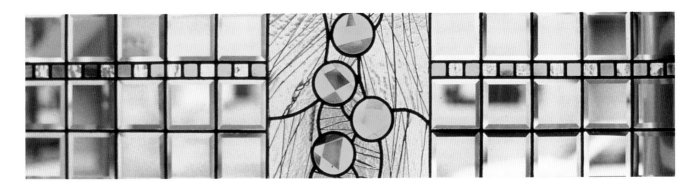

WINDOW
Beveled optical lenses with random facets,
Asahi opal glass, antique clear glass
36" x 12" (91 cm x 30 cm)

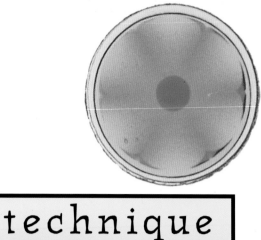

technique

Larry Zgoda

I design panels to be compatible with the buildings they occupy. I also consider how the design form will work with the physical structure of the panel, because the piece needs to withstand whatever may come along. The structure needs to be strong enough to be there a hundred years from now, and I want the design to be as appropriate then as when I first created it.

My designs are affected foremost by available light. I work with subtle colors, and clear and white glasses. The light affects where and how I place different types and colors of glass, and I often take samples to the site to see how they will catch the light. I incorporate bevels to bend the view through the panel and to alter the light coming through the panel.

In constructing a panel, I like to be conservative. I create the initial sketch by putting in the reinforcing bar lines, constructing the lead

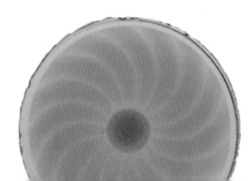

lines of the design afterward. I use a flat reinforcing bar, so that the width is no greater than that of the lead lines in the window. I like to establish a foundation of very predictable geometry, usually on the lower portion of a window, and then let go with a wilder design on the upper portion. This predictable base is a way for me to work in structural considerations, while providing a visual anchor to the panel. It also allows me to use large unbroken panes of fairly nondescript glass to contrast with smaller, colored beveled pieces. This contrast is key to my designs; it makes the colors and planes of the beveled pieces come alive.

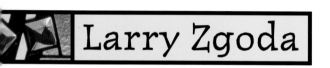

Larry Zgoda

WINDOW
Austrian crystal jewels cut and faceted into triangles,
beveled wire-glass squares, clear glass
24" x 66" (61 cm x 168 cm)

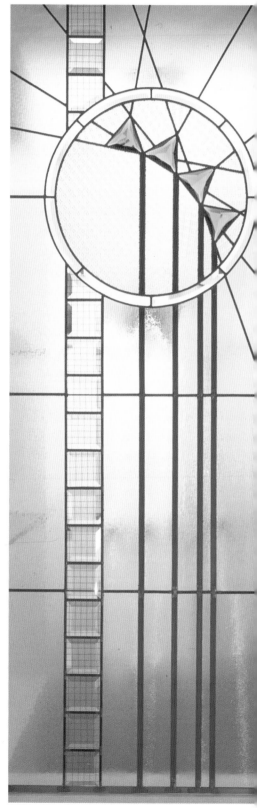

WINDOW
Beveled clear glass, custom-beveled
wire-glass squares and circles
30" x 14" (76 cm x 36 cm)

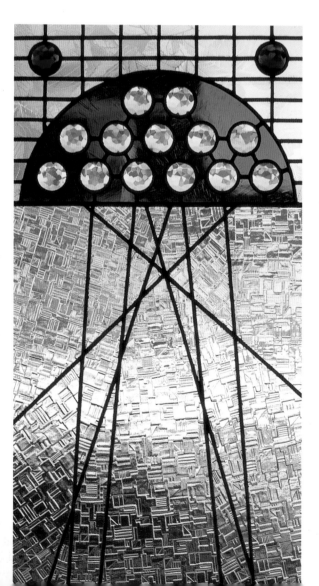

WINDOW
Blue glass oval inset with
antique beveled jewels,
machined glass, cut pink jewels
16" x 30" (41 cm x 76 cm)

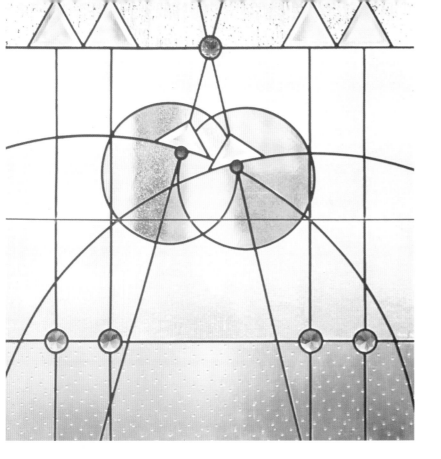

CASEMENT WINDOW
Asahi blue-opal beveled jewels, beveled triangles,
ruby faceted jewels, stained glass, machined glass
31" x 33" (79 cm x 84 cm)

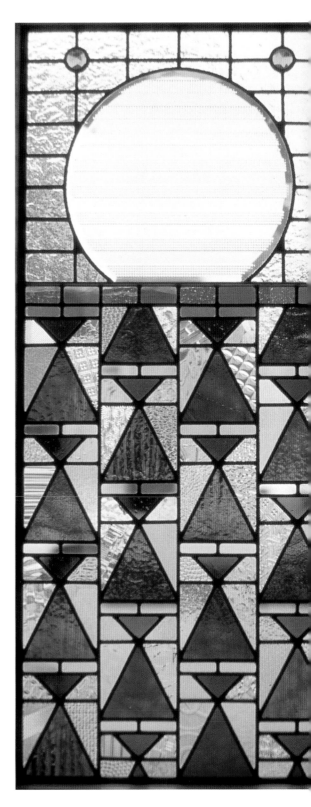

WINDOW
Christmas
Beveled, textured glass circle, gold antique jewels, gold
antique glass, gold ruby-stained glass, hand rolled clear glass
16" x 36" (41 cm x 91 cm)

AUTONOMOUS PANEL (detail)
Beveled clear glass triangles, cut gold-pink jewels, custom-beveled
peach plate, beveled on opposite sides (cube)
14" x 16" (36 cm x 41 cm)

The pursuit of glass as art and career was a logical evolution for Shelley Jurs, marking the

Shelley Jurs

culmination of an interest in hands-on arts and crafts dating from childhood. She was an art major in college, eventually transferring to the renown California College of Arts and Crafts. Focusing on ceramics, Jurs explored a range of other media as well. An invitation from her brother-in-law to spend the summer working at his glass studio marked a turning point. As a result, she left school to work in the studio full-time.

Two years later, seeking to explore and expand upon her own glass design sensibilities, Jurs attended the Swansea College of Art in South Wales. She then became a personal assistant to legendary German glass artist

DESIGN SERIES DOOR
Handblown textured and clear glasses, hand-cast jewels
3' x 6.8' (.9 m x 2.1 m)

Ludwig Shaffrath, an essential influence on the development of Jurs's own style in glass. Shaffrath taught her the importance of using the line as a defining graphic element.

Jurs emphasizes her line work through the clean angles of the cast beveled pieces she so often uses. She intentionally avoids bold splashes of color, opting instead for the soothing and meditative elegance of neutral colors and clear and textured glasses. Her goal is to create an uplifting space for the viewers of the work; light and its transition through the glass are key principle concerns in achieving that goal.

DOOR
Diamond Heights
Handblown glass, cast jewels, in steel frame
3' x 8' (.9 m x 2.4 m)

Bevels and glass jewels have become a trademark of my work for many reasons. I enjoy how the repetition of simple geometric modules creates new, expanded forms of expression, and I prize the illusion of depth and layered light that beveled glass offers. In addition, the creation of color through the use of no color—taking advantage of the prismatic qualities of the bevel—reminds me of some mystical life force.

In taking advantage of this potential, I have become more and more involved with integrating structure. Structure and design can be unified to create a wonderful style. As with wood, steel, aluminum, and lead came, or other framing components that join and contain the glass pieces, essential structural elements must become integral parts of the design. In contemplating a design, I may engage an engineer or other specialist to ensure these issues

are being dealt with so that the piece functions structurally. That's simply part of my design process. This is in keeping with a basic technical philosophy of creating works to last. I don't believe in pushing materials beyond their innate ability merely for the benefit of some tricky technique that eventually causes the physical breakdown of the original expression. There must always be a marriage between materials and design, one that endures through time.

Shelley Jurs

MOUNTED DOOR
Ninelite
Handblown glass and hand-cast glass jewels
32" x 6.8' (81 cm x 2.1 m)

DOUBLE DOORS
Handblown and hand-cast glass jewels, bevels
6' x 8' (1.8 m x 2.4 m)

BATHROOM WINDOWS (opposite)
Radiant Light
Handblown glass and cast beveled jewels
6' x 8' (1.8 m x 2.4 m)

DOME SKYLIGHT
Celestial Phenomena
Handblown seedy and reamy glasses
and hand-cast jewels, bevels
22' (6.7 m) in diameter

DOUBLE DOORS
Black lacquer frame, beveled and round
jewels, clear and textured glasses
5' x 7' (1.5 m x 2.1 m)

Kenneth vonRoenn's training as an architect gives

him a unique perspective on the potential of, and

unique

consider-

ations

inherent

Kenneth vonRoenn

in, glass art. In 1991, he purchased the studio where

he began his glass art career, giving him the control

to select commissions that focus on considerations of

interest to him, such as the way light entering a

space affects the occupants of that space.

VonRoenn's experience gives him an insider's

understanding of how a glass design relates to the

larger environment. In creating a panel, he considers

how the space will be used, how often—and for how

long—the viewer will be exposed to the piece, and

what overall tone the architecture sets. He focuses

on completing the architecture, making it more

memorable, exciting, and interesting than it would

be without the glass art.

Over the last decade, vonRoenn has increasingly used bevels in his pieces. Beyond the prismatic effects such elements provide, he is attracted to the ability of bevels to fracture the image as seen through the panel, creating an impressionistic sense. He uses bevels to elevate the sense of color and the character of the light, making the inanimate articulate and adding expression to the environment. VonRoenn's work adds an intellectual lyricism to the static combination of building materials. It provides thoughtful poetry in glass, food as much for the soul and mind as for the eye.

GLASS COLUMNS, UNIVERSITY OF TOLEDO
(detail showing the complexity and chaos
of the overlaid forms)

GLASS COLUMNS,
UNIVERSITY OF TOLEDO (opposite)
Layers of beveled clear and stained glasses create a form
that becomes less understandable the closer the viewer gets.
10' x 24" (3 m x 61 cm)

technique

Kenneth vonRoenn

Structure is as critical as aesthetics within architectural art. I try to solve the fundamental issues of structure relatively early in design development. These initial structural considerations do not in any way lessen my enthusiasm for the project. In fact, I find that the exploration of structure—the eventual construction of the work of art—informs my aesthetics.

In the initial stages of creating the design, I look at the options and choose the best possible structural choices for the panel on which I'm working. I take into account the panel's exposure, its size, and its environment—where it will be placed. I keep the concerns in mind right through to actual fabrication.

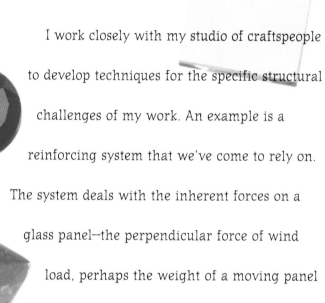

I work closely with my studio of craftspeople to develop techniques for the specific structural challenges of my work. An example is a reinforcing system that we've come to rely on. The system deals with the inherent forces on a glass panel—the perpendicular force of wind load, perhaps the weight of a moving panel within a door, and the secondary force of gravity. We organize our reinforcing bars to counteract those forces by positioning bars horizontally on one surface and vertically on another, and anchoring them securely to the frame. By developing solutions specific to each of my projects, my art, like the buildings in which it is situated, will stand the test of time.

Kenneth vonRoenn

DOORS
Straight-line bevels laminated end-to-end,
stained glass, textured glass
2'1"x 6'8" (.6 m x 2.1 m)
each door

GLASS SCULPTURAL COLUMN
Stained and clear glasses
12' x 12" x 12" (3.7 m x 30 cm x 30 cm)

ENTRYWAY
Straight-line bevels, round glass
jewels, stained glass, clear glass
8' x 8' (2.4 m x 2.4 m)

Carl Powell considers the limitations of the medium of glass art as challenges to his talent.

He refuses to let the traditional or the accepted way of doing things confine his vision. His background as a painter drives him to create unusual and original optical effects rarely found in glass art. Twenty-five years ago, as a student of painting, he came across photographs of the stunning stained glass work of the painter Joseph Albers. That discovery led him to take a summer job in a stained glass studio.

Powell explored beveling as an opportunity to create a new interplay of shapes and textures. Crafted in colorless glass, his beveled pieces started as a way to escape the confines of studio commissions, where clients wanted pieces to include every color of the rainbow. After Powell moved to California, a client asked him to create a piece in his signature style, but including some

color. He reintroduced color on his own terms, using bold but limited splashes of vibrant hues against large fields of clear and textured glasses.

Powell's unconventional style combines beveled polygons, cylinders, and cubes with shadowy textured glass and vibrant shocks of color. His innovative approach to his art does not stop with his style. He often creates works in multiple panels that the client can rearrange to suit his or her personal preference. But true to their nature, his works never lose the balance of chaos and control that is so much their hallmark.

WINDOW (opposite)
Carnival
Pale blue and white creamy antique handblown German glasses, beveled shapes including cylinders, discs, and cubes
10' x 6' (3 m x 1.8 m)

PENTHOUSE WINDOW (detail, above)
Untitled
Clear background glass textured to provide privacy, stained glass, machined glass, beveled shapes
17' x 2' (5.2 m x .6 m) total window

technique

Carl Powell

I began beveling as a way to depart from the traditional confines of stained glass design, and the techniques I use evolved from there. After a while, it was important to me to be able to do something different, without being told how it had to be done.

I became interested in the shapes you can create by beveling on both sides, causing them to appear much thicker than they really are, like optical illusions. I like to take long pieces of thick glass and just multifacet the whole surface. Then, when you walk in front of the finished piece, it really becomes kinetic, capturing colors from the outside environment and making them dance across the surface of the glass. Another technique I use to create a drawing effect is overleading, where I run lead right over the glass and just stop it, without going to another piece of lead.

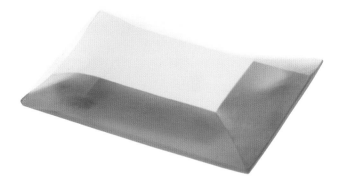

These techniques are ways to expand my glass

vocabulary. I think the artist has to continually

search for new ways to express meaning in his or

her work. The flexibility I've found in beveling

allows me that exploration, in much

the same way that a painter

uses his paints.

Carl Powell

FREESTANDING SCREEN
Navigator
Variety of textured and clear glasses,
stained glass, and beveled shapes
7' x 5.5' (2.1 m x 1.7 m)

Navigator (detail)
This portion of the screen shows the optical illusions created by beveling
on both sides of a piece of glass. The heart is a fully beveled piece that
broke and was then cut, beveled, rejoined, and leaded into the screen.

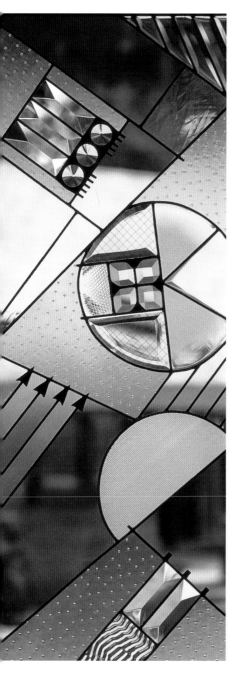

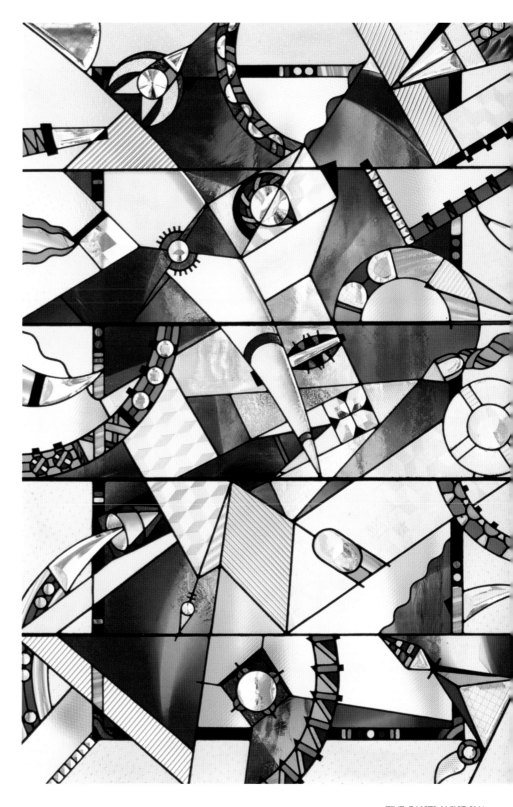

GLASS DOOR ENTRYWAY
Untitled
Beveled 1.25" (3.5 cm) glass to create a prismatic
effect, and arrows created by overlaying lead on
the glass
6' x 2.5' (1.8 m x .8 m)

FIVE-PANEL WINDOW
Flamenco in Cobalt
Variegated cobalt German handblown glass, extensive
beveling throughout, steel frame around each section
11' x 8' (3.4 m x 2.4 m)

Virginia Hoffman's design skills were well developed by the time she found her way into

Virginia Hoffman

the world of glass art.

Shortly after graduating from college with a degree in graphic design, she veered off her career path in advertising to take a job at a local stained glass studio. Her design skills and talents, honed in the two-dimensional world of paper, were vividly translated into seductive three-dimensional form.

Drawing on her eclectic interests that range from mid-century abstract expressionists to the German Bauhaus movement and beyond, Hoffman has created a fluid yet dynamic style that seems to transcend the material in which she works. Most of the bevels she uses are custom shaped to her specifications. These

ENTRYWAY DOORS
(detail showing the curved and pyramid peak bevels and textured background glasses)

oddly shaped, curved pieces offer the allure of a facet without interrupting the flow of the design.

Hoffman uses her bevels to their best advantage, accentuating their sharp clarity with complementary clear and textured glasses. She limits her use of colors, rarely incorporating more than one in any given piece. In Hoffman's work, the simplicity of sound design transcends the complexity of a crowded palette.

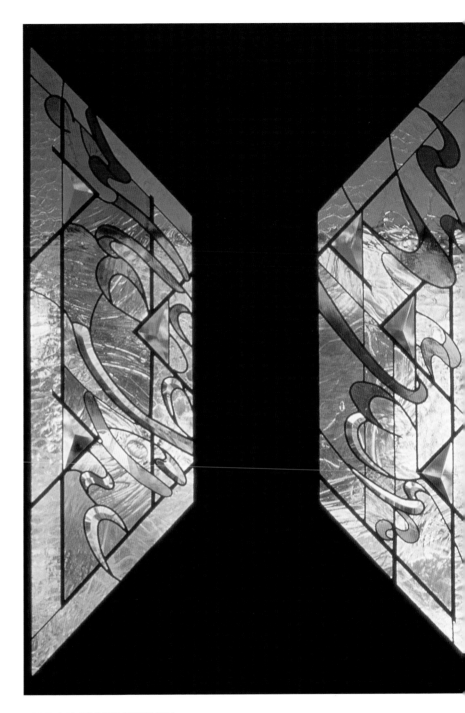

DOUBLE PANELS FOR ENTRYWAY
Reamy clear glass, crackle glass, pink-gold stained glass
45" x 65" (114 cm x 165 cm)

One of the more interesting challenges in creating the type of panels I design is disguising the structural elements within the design. Standard steel reinforcing bar—rebar, as it is called—is rigid and extremely difficult to incorporate into curvy lines. For that reason, I often use zinc reinforcing bars, which can be bent much more easily than traditional steel bars.

A second—and even greater—challenge was finding someone to custom bevel pieces of glass to

technique

Virginia Hoffman

my specifications. My work is abstract and fluid, and I usually don't want to use straight, mass-produced bevels. Putting a facet on an uneven or oddly shaped piece of glass is no easy task. I was lucky enough to find a master beveler named Dan Woodward in Portland, Oregon. We have worked together quite well, and Dan has been able to execute bevels to the most difficult specifications I can imagine.

Many times, I draw a design and actually place the peak of the bevel so that it complements the lines in the design. This sort of visual interest is key to what I do. Having a relationship with a beveler who is able to do that type of exacting work greatly expands the possibilities of using bevels in my work.

Virginia Hoffman

WINDOW
German handblown glass, straight-line stock bevels, beveled pyramids
58" x 63" (147 cm x 160 cm)

DOUBLE DOORS AND ARCH-TOP WINDOW
Desag antique thick glass used for bevels, stained glass,
reamy used in background glass
6' x 15' (1.8 m x 4.6 m)

STAINED GLASS WALL, CORPORATE BUILDING
Flemish Pilkington clear textured glass,
Fremont stained glass, and beveled circles
8' x 11' (2.4 m x 3.4 m)

FIREPLACE SCREEN
Beveled thick glass, blue
acid-etched glass,
machined glass
45" x 65" (114 cm x 165 cm)
(detail, above, showing
the extremely difficult
beveled curved pieces
and the acid-etched
blue glass)

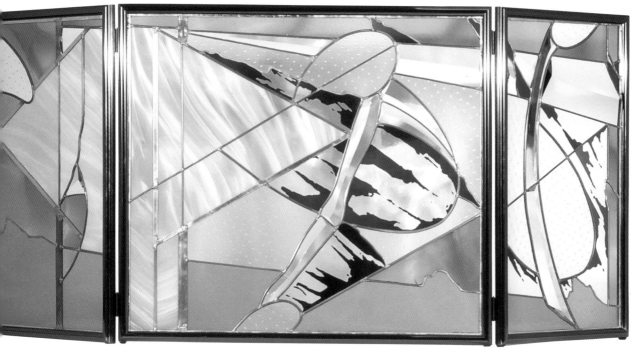

PAINTED GLASS
FRAGILE BRUSHSTROKES

Painting on stained glass is an adventure in the modulation of light and color unlike any other medium. The artist controls the translucency of color and line and can, if they so choose, escape the traditional confines of the lead line by painting on an unbroken panel of glass, or by crossing the lead line with the painting itself. Traditionally done by laying down a thick matte of paint and cutting form out of that, modern glass painters have adapted materials and techniques to suit their own styles and to create works amazingly original in conception and execution.

Serving as a bridge between old and new in both techniques and style, master glass painter Patrick Reyntiens executes designs combining an amazingly refined eye for color with unparalleled wit and insight. His philosophical approach and dynamic style have inspired numerous artists, including Ellen Mandelbaum. Mandelbaum has long since followed her own muse to develop a boldly distinctive style. She creates beautiful panels with organic and free-flowing forms.

Linda Lichtman
INDEPENDENT PANEL (detail, above)
Inside the Outside
Vitreous paint, acid-etched,
stained, and leaded glasses
11" x 16" (28 cm x 41 cm)

Linda Lichtman has chosen a more colorful and often figural style. Her whimsical and upbeat representations contrast starkly with her darkly dramatic colors. British painter Debora Coombs shares this sense of color. She explores the universal themes of the human condition with striking sensitivity all the more amazing given her mathematical predilections.

Marie Foucault's wild and uninhibited brushwork illuminates the stories and personal revelations that take form on all of her panels. Mary Mackey also allows her brush free rein as she finds her style moving away from the figural and into a more expressionistic realm.

Patrick Reyntiens
ONE OF EIGHT INDEPENDENT "CIRCUS" RONDELS
Clown Piece
German, French, and English antique glasses,
painted *alla prima* using matte and rapid brushstrokes
29" (74 cm) in diameter

Patrick Reyntiens

Master glass painter Patrick Reyntiens has inspired and educated generations of stained glass artists. He has been essential in helping to expand the range and vocabulary of the art in both Europe and America. His book, *The Technique of Stained Glass*, is considered the seminal text on the art. Reyntiens's myriad accomplishments include extensive writings on a range of subjects and commissions throughout Europe and America. But as impressive as this resume might be, it falls second to his refined skill as a painter and glass artist, exhibited in his unerring control of color and light.

That use of color is the first element the viewer notices. Even to the untrained eye, a panel

WINDOW (detail)
Twelve Heads of Dame Edna
German, French, and antique glasses
55" x 29" (140 cm x 74 cm)

painted by Reyntiens is a visual feast—luscious, enigmatic, and satisfying. He works in a vivid spectrum of related colors, balancing intensity, value, and hue so that the entire work is unified. In *Hommage à Fauré*, a cornucopia of colors mesh in such a vibrant, charismatic image that it seems contradictory to call the work a still life.

This animation characterizes Reyntiens's work, from figurative pieces that call to mind the masterpieces of medieval times to the witty and sparkling images of a more contemporary bent. His purposeful and confident use of color, and the synthesis of that color with lines of paint and lead, remain unmatched among glass painters.

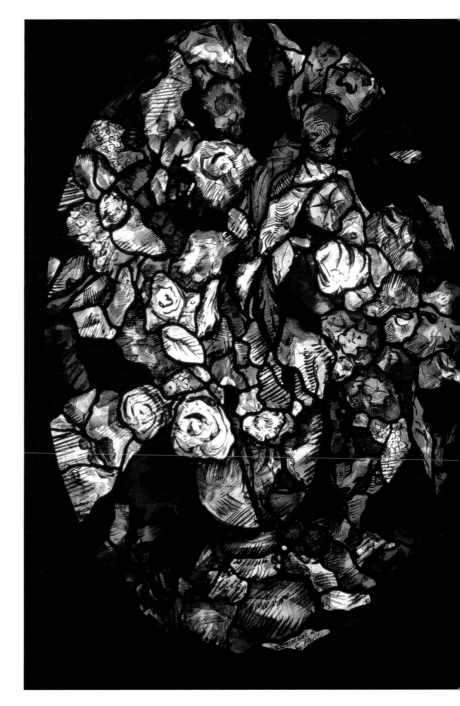

INDEPENDENT PANEL
Hommage à Fauré
German, French, and antique glasses
39" x 28" (99 cm x 71 cm)

technique

Patrick Reyntiens

I'm not a technical wizard, as such. Expression and artistic intent must take precedence over mere technical cleverness. If you do a thing, from riding a bicycle to going to the moon, you must find the right way of doing it.

A major challenge early on was the Baptistery Window at Coventry Cathedral. I had to do an enormous John Piper watercolor in glass. It was 82 feet high by 55 feet wide (25 meters high by 16.8 meters wide), presenting an unusual first "trial by fire." The top of the window was to be different blues that needed to have a common element when lit. I discovered in London a source of "railroad" glass, a turquoise blue mechanical

glass of uniform color. I plated the glass to the window and laid down the varied blues of the design on top of it. The railroad glass acted as a subtle unifying tone, yet it was not discernible to the eye.

Glass painters in particular need to play with transparency versus translucency. I've always worked in glass as a painter, rather than as a craftsman, and my glass expression depends on the exploration between translucency and transparency. I think you need to move quickly and assertively, which is why I have always painted very fast. I believe it is the only way to make a piece have sparkle, verve, and a life of its own.

Patrick Reyntiens

WINDOW IN MACAULEY HOUSE APSE, ENGLAND
Commercial factory glass, German antique glass,
alla prima painting, slumping
11' x 16.5' (3.4 m x 5 m)

ONE OF TWELVE WINDOWS
The Last Labor of Hercules
German, French, and English antique glasses
16.5" x 15" (42 cm x 38 cm)

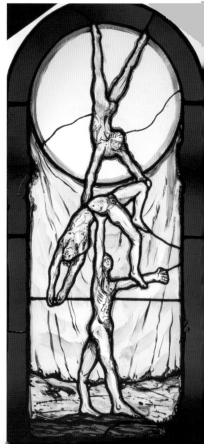

INDEPENDENT PANEL
Homage to the Olympiads
Alla prima painting (some pieces of
glass are plated to get an exact
nuance of expression in the color)
42" x 20.5" (107 cm x 52 cm)

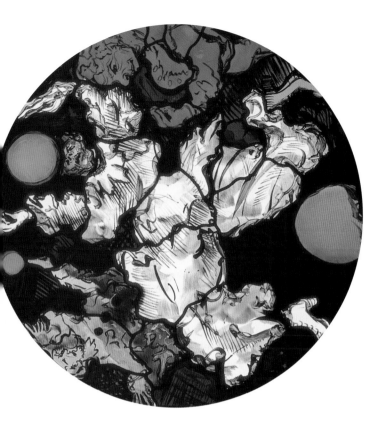

ONE OF EIGHT INDEPENDENT "CIRCUS" RONDELS
Ball Balance
German, French, and English antique glasses,
painted *alla prima* using matte and rapid brushstrokes
29" (74 cm) in diameter

ONE OF TWELVE WINDOWS
The Tenth Labor of Hercules
German, French, and English antique glasses,
painting and staining, with etching and plating
16.5" x 15" (42 cm x 38 cm)

ONE OF EIGHT INDEPENDENT "CIRCUS" RONDELS
A Pretty Balance
German, French, and English antique glasses,
painted *alla prima* using matte and rapid brushstrokes
29" (74 cm) in diameter

Ellen Mandelbaum's training and talent as a painter on canvas were essential to her develop-

Ellen Mandelbaum

ment as a glass painter. She uses her grounding in traditional brushwork to explore the novel and varied ways glass and light can affect the viewer's perception of her painted images.

Glass art offers other attractions as well. Mandelbaum enjoys the physical act of working on a piece of glass. She finds that light passing through glass makes the experience different from painting on canvas or paper. Working with glass also gives her the chance to explore architectural considerations, something that has always interested her. And perhaps most important, with glass art, Mandelbaum has the opportunity to create a piece that intimately affects the work's

owner; through this medium, she has discovered a level of personal contact she had not encountered before.

So almost from the start, Mandelbaum believed in the power of painted glass. Using a style ripe with nuance and inflected with almost constant references to nature, she creates art that truly matters. The honesty of each flowing brushstroke has a profound value and impact. To Mandelbaum, her work has the ability to transform simple light into a thing of greater beauty and to transform the lives of those who come in contact with it.

INDEPENDENT PANEL
MOUNTED IN WINDOW
Southampton Waves
Black paint, silk-screening,
reamy and antique glasses
21" x 46" (53 cm x 117 cm)

technique

Ellen Mandelbaum

One of my favorite parts of painting on glass is the actual painting, having the freedom of the brushstroke and being able to invent as I go. Traditionally, artists divide glass painting into matting and tracing, first putting down a general tone, and then creating a thin line. I do them together, which is a little more like regular painting in a way. But that is not to say that painting on glass is like painting on any other surface—it is a radically different thing. I love to put down tone and blend using a wide brush; then I scratch through and release the light. That part is so wonderful, and it is not like any other painting in the world.

The material itself is different as well. Glass paints are metal oxides. To use them, you mix in a little gum arabic—the same glue that holds watercolor together—and, in my case, some water.

I love the way glass paint flows over the surface of the glass, and I sometimes use reamy glass for this very effect. Painting is the one technique in which you really get a sense of the human touch. This is very evident in my work on *Grisaille Oval*, a piece I painted again and again. The painting was kind of pure and wonderful, and represents the potential for expression that exists in glass painting.

Ellen Mandelbaum

INDEPENDENT PANEL
Grisaille Oval
Grisaille brown, umber, black, and red
for flesh paints, on drawn antique glass
15" x 16" (38 cm x 41 cm)

WINDOW
Untitled
Black paint and silver stain, Fremont white-on-clear
wispy glass at center, French ruby glass, fluted glass
26" x 40" (66 cm x 102 cm)

ENTRYWAY SIDELIGHTS
(opposite and detail, left)
Untitled
Grisaille paints and silver
stain, antique glass
above, squares of
machine-rolled opales-
cent streaky glass below
16" x 70" (41 cm x 178 cm)
each

INDEPENDENT PANEL MOUNTED IN WINDOW
Wales Waterfall
Black and blue paint, antique blue and colored glasses
12" x 15" (30 cm x 38 cm)

INDEPENDENT PANEL
Imaginary Landscape
Black paint and ivory enamel, pure red, blue,
and light blue French mouthblown glasses
76" x 14" (193 cm x 36 cm)

ENTRYWAY SIDELIGHTS
Untitled
Grisaille paints and silver stain, antique glass
above, squares of machine-rolled opalescent
streaky glass below
16" x 70" (41 cm x 178 cm) each

Linda Lichtman's rich imagery challenges the viewer to shed traditional audience passivity

Linda Lichtman

and engage her vibrant choreography of dark jewel colors and assertive lines. Through her art, she strives to communicate a sense of the emotional content of her images.

The whipsaw movement and often surreal nature of Lichtman's luscious textural work invite intense exploration. Her painted glass art is driven by a palpable energy, a magical force derived from the balanced tension between openness and opacity, between the rigid framework of the lead line and the dynamic nature of Lichtman's brushwork.

INDEPENDENT PANEL
Snake in the Glass
Vitreous paint and silver stains, acid-etched stained glass
32" x 11" (81 cm x 28 cm)

That duality—between what is seen and what is not, between the physical and the spiritual, between compartments defined by lead lines and the free flow of imagery—adds life and vigor to Lichtman's work. Her commissions, such as *Tree of Knowledge, Tree of Light*, tend to be more transparent, with generous open areas. In contrast, her autonomous panels, such as *Primary Ties*, are more fluid, concentrated, and opaque. In both cases, Lichtman continually brings new and vital interpretations to the timeless technique of glass painting.

WINDOW
Family of Fish
Vitreous paint, enamels, and silver stains, acid-etched, laminated, and engraved stained glasses
43" x 13" (109 cm x 33 cm)

technique
Linda Lichtman

As beautiful as it is, stained glass, straight from the manufacturer, bores and challenges me. The excitement for me begins with tearing into the glass, whether with a Dremel engraver, acid etching, or paint. I can actually proceed almost as with a drawing, to have my hand in there making an imprint on the glass.

I like to literally and figuratively peel away a layer and reveal something underneath, which is why I often use flashed glass, where one color of glass is superimposed upon a layer of another color or clear glass. Acid etching flashed glass allows me to control how much of the color I leave on and how strong the color will be. Using acid in this way is almost another way to paint.

I like the fact that I'm using a material that can be seen as very rigid and cold—in a way, unresponsive and ungiving—and that I find ways of

making it more expressive and bending it to my will. Some of this also has to do with my own temperament. Spontaneity is a key to my expressive style, and without it, I can become quite frustrated. With painting and acid etching, I get results that I am able to modify fairly easily. Ultimately, I work to expand the possibilities of the material itself, to penetrate and engage it using the human touch and, thereby, to touch the viewer.

Linda Lichtman

INDEPENDENT PANEL
Primary Ties
Vitreous paints and enamels, acid-etched and sandblasted
stained glasses, welded rebar and lead-wire frame
9" x 12" (23 cm x 30 cm)

LIBRARY WINDOW
Tree of Knowledge, Tree of Light
Vitreous paints, enamels, and silver stains,
acid-etched stained glass and float glass, leaded
and laminated
3.5' x 12' (1.1 m x 3.7 m)

INDEPENDENT PANEL (above)
Fish Flow, Lava Flow
Vitreous paints, acid-etched stained glass
22" x 12" (56 cm x 30 cm)

INDEPENDENT PANEL (below)
Waxing Germanic
Vitreous paints applied with wax resist,
acid-etched stained glass
16" x 12" (41 cm x 30 cm)

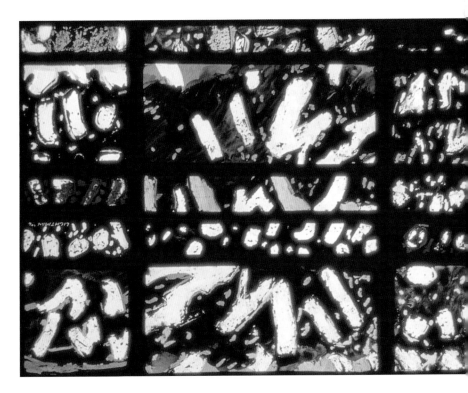

ONE OF SIX EXHIBITION PIECES (detail)
Six Land Escapes
Vitreous paints and enamels, acid-etched,
engraved, and laminated stained glasses,
steel wire and hardwood frame
36" x 8'4" (91 cm x 2.6 m)

Artist Debora Coombs has combined the seemingly incompatible worlds of precise, scientific

Debora Coombs

geometry and warm, fluid organic form. Using the traditional technique of painting glass in most untraditional ways, Coombs creates artwork that invites the viewer to explore tier after tier of messages and meanings.

Coombs presents these meanings in many ways, ranging from semiabstract pieces to figural works to richly embellished geometric patterns. Regardless of the form, the spiritual dimension of her work and the humanity of her expressive painted lines cannot be denied.

Coombs's work possesses a metaphysical depth found both in the construction of each

EXHIBITION PIECE, IN THE COLLECTION OF
THE STAINED GLASS MUSEUM, ELY CATHEDRAL, ENGLAND
Out of Confusion . . .
Painted and stained glasses
78" x 52.5" (198 cm x 133 cm)

piece and in the often mathematical reasoning behind it. Coombs designed the window, *Out of Confusion . . .* based on the floor plan of St. Mary's Chapel in Glastonbury, Great Britain. She used this pattern to represent an internal narrative, with colors depicting emotions contained by black borders. Through this kind of art, Coombs elevates the glass painter's craft to the level of eternal and ethereal expression.

GALLERY EXHIBITION PIECE FROM THE SERIES "ONE WOMAN'S NARRATIVE,"
FROM THE COLLECTION OF CHRISTOPHER POWELL, ENGLAND
Blue Dog Daughters
Painted and stained glasses
15.5" x 23.25" (39 cm x 59 cm)

technique

Debora Coombs

Glass painting has a centuries-old tradition in Europe, and I am always aware of that tradition, that I am working in a medium rich with history. Just the same, my own glass painting is extremely idiosyncratic. The style and manner of application are something that I've worked out myself through extensive experimentation.

Each new project challenges me to increase my repertoire of mark-making, my glass-painting vocabulary.

I like to get right into the paint. I find the material, the actual paint, very alluring. I often use my hands and get right in up to my elbows. I learned early on that you have to develop a certain immediacy and confidence with glass. Glass painting can easily look like dirty smudges. You need good opacity, and you need to get it right the first time

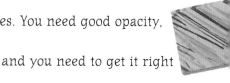

so that the work has a sense of

spontaneity and liveliness.

I think we are all born with our own

"hand," our own innate style that develops and

matures over the years. Like calligraphy, glass

painting is something you do with your whole

mind and body; it is affected by the way you stand,

how you hold yourself, the way you breathe, and

the way gravity draws the paint down on the

brush. It's a fascinating balance of control of

the uncontrollable, which is certainly one of the

things I love best about painting on glass.

GALLERY EXHIBITION PIECE FROM THE SERIES
"ONE WOMAN'S NARRATIVE"
Self Portrait IV
Painted stained glass
12" x 8" (30 cm x 20 cm)

ENTRANCE FOYER WINDOW, ITCHEN COLLEGE
Ways of Seeing
Painted stained glass
3' 11" (.94 m) in diameter

STAINED GLASS WINDOW, WESTBOROUGH HIG
SCHOOL, DEWSBURY, ENGLAN
Painted, stained, and clear textured glass
9.1' x 17' (2.7 m x 5.2 r

Debora Coombs

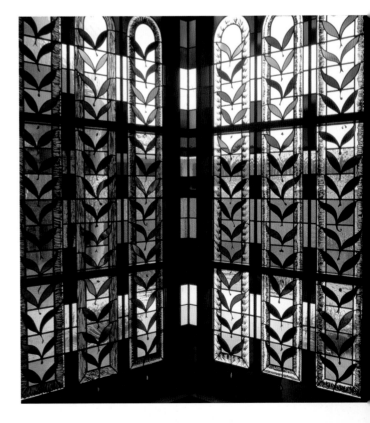

GALLERY EXHIBITION PIECE FROM THE SERIES
"ONE WOMAN'S NARRATIVE"
Collection of Dr. Gordon Bowe, Dublin, Ireland
Woman
Painted stained glass
15.5" x 23.25" (39 cm x 59 cm)

EXHIBITION PIECE
Inner Room
Painted stained glass
4.3' x 17" (1.3 m x 43 cm)

GALLERY EXHIBITION
PIECE FROM THE SERIES
"ONE WOMAN'S
NARRATIVE"
Young Willows . . .
Painted stained glass
15.5" x 23.25"
(39 cm x 59 cm)

Free spirit Marie Foucault challenges the traditions in which she was so thoroughly trained. A little

over two decades ago, she graduated from the elite French National Superior School of Applied Arts and Crafts. She began a career as a highly regarded conservationist, a professional at restoring stained glass windows dating from the thirteenth to the sixteenth centuries. Although she achieved a mastery of antiquity, her passion lay in creating groundbreaking contemporary work.

Foucault willingly questions everything about her medium, including whether she needs to include lead lines. She works more and more on full sheets of clear and blown glasses, using a variety of paints to create what she would call "a new vocabulary." In a world where painted stained glass is poorly understood at best,

pushing the envelope of this form is risky. Yet Foucault has the faith of the talented.

Her confidence is apparent in every animated brushstroke and in every wild layer that forms an alliance with light. Foucault's work is fearless and overwhelming, so much a departure from her roots that you might think she has shed her past. But her beginnings set the stage for her current work. Foucault's creations represent a response to artistic freedom, celebrated in grand and glorious color and unrestrained line.

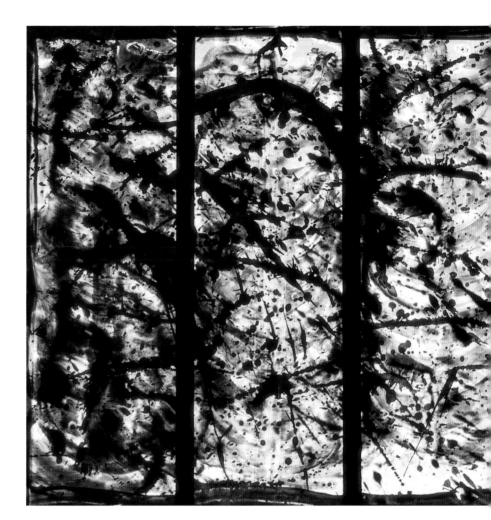

INDEPENDENT PANEL
Shroud
Blue grisaille, silver stain overfired, panel composed of six pieces of clear glass, painted on both sides and plated together to form a three-piece glass panel
20.25" x 21" (51 cm x 53 cm)

INDEPENDENT PANEL (opposite)
Tsunami
Blue and black grisaille on .25" plate glass
20" x 15" (51 cm x 38 cm)

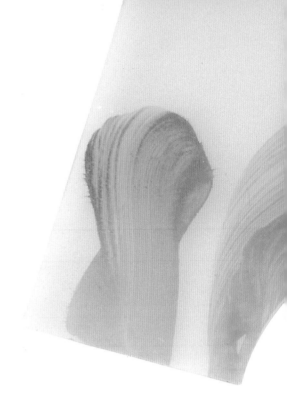

technique

Marie Foucault

There is no escaping the fact that I learned
the techniques of painting and leaded
glasswork in a most traditional fashion.
My current work is indebted to the skills
I acquired in learning to do—and doing—
restoration work. But now I am willing
to try the unusual and look for possibilities
in everything. I hold no prejudices, even
about the material itself. I sometimes use
clear glass—chipped, scratched, damaged,

or found on the streets of New York. Suddenly, it is on the light table and under my brush, rich with grisaille paint, a new story being written.

An area where my work is expanding is in the use of silver stains. In past centuries, stains were used on the back of glass to color areas of architecture, hair, draperies, and other fine details.

Silver stain is generally fired at 1,050 degrees Fahrenheit. At higher temperatures, the silver in the stain "metalizes," creating a wild range of colors and iridescence. I love the iridescent quality, so I always fire my silver stain up to 1,150 or even 1,200 degrees Fahrenheit. As I use silver stain on the front of my work, the effect can be seen at night, with reflective light creating a completely different panel than the one seen during the day.

THREE SLIDING PANELS IN A SCREEN
Shadows of Reflection Triptych
Dark blue and white grisaille, orange silver
stain, French and German antique glasses
13' x 8'5" (4 m x 2.6 m)

Marie Foucault

INDEPENDENT PANEL
Glass Kimono
Brown and black grisaille,
silver stain, clear window glass
15" x 20" (38 cm x 51 cm)

INDEPENDENT PANEL
Blue Damage
Blue and black grisaille, silver stain, clear restoration glass
21.5" x 18.5" (55 cm x 47 cm)

PANEL IN A
DOUBLE-HUNG WINDOW
The Cat and the Owl
Grisaille, French and
German antique glasses
48" x 35" (122 cm x 89 cm)

INDEPENDENT PANEL
FOR EXHIBITION
I Got the Blues
Blue and black grisaille,
silver stain, clear
window glass
12" (30 cm) square

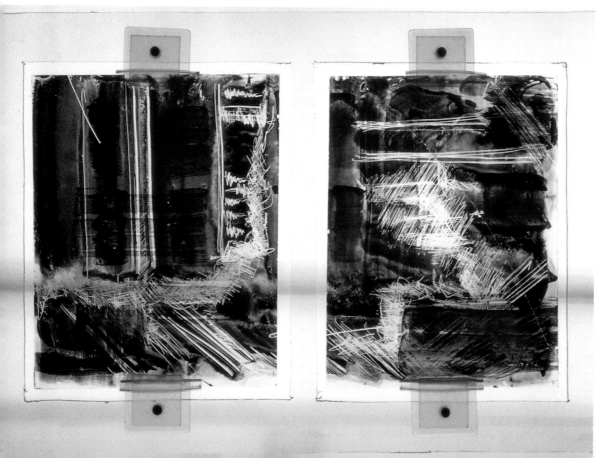

Irish artist Mary Mackey uses color as an ethereal expression rather than as a tool. Her brilliant,

magical hues become even more radiant when punctuated by her kinetic line work. Her homeland serves as a chief influence, specifically the dramatic lighting and varied shades of Ireland.

Mackey first focused on the power of color during her studies at Crawford College of Art and Design in Ireland. After graduating as a painter, she began to work in stained glass, a medium in which she saw great potential. But her emphasis on this medium does not mean she has left other forms of painting behind. In fact, Mackey uses one discipline to balance and support the other. Her work with the same technique in different media allows her to explore themes in various arenas.

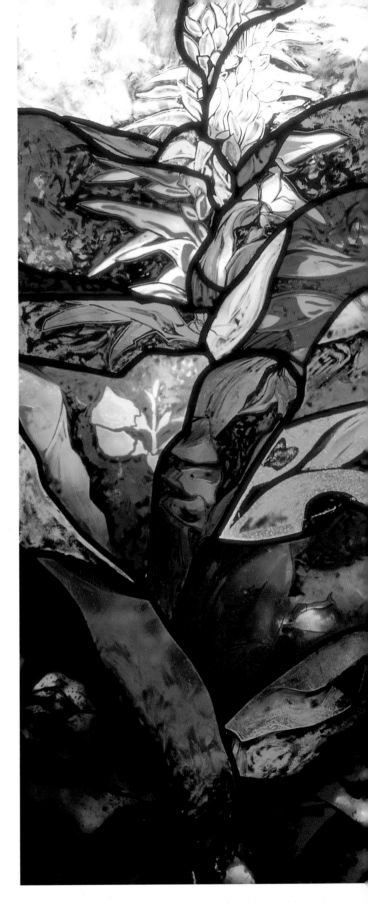

INDEPENDENT PANEL MOUNTED IN WINDOW
(above and detail, opposite)
Liquid Layers
Painted stained glass
17" x 38.5" (43 cm x 98 cm)

This interaction has led her to move from largely figural work to a more abstract vocabulary in her glass painting.

Mackey's recent work focuses less on structure and more on impressions and experience. Through her enigmatic use of color and layered shading and line, she attempts to communicate emotions and sensations. Removed from the perspective of literal imagery, she freely wanders through larger themes, exploring what the paint itself can contribute, and how best to orchestrate the timeless dance of intense color and vibrant light.

Acid etching is an essential technique
in my work, especially my more recent pieces.
Before I start, I have an idea of where I'm going
to etch, so that I do some areas quite strongly and
barely touch others. Generally, I leave the panel
unprotected and use a small dropper bottle to
squeeze a little acid in certain areas. I then spray
a little water on the panel to
push the acid out to the edge.
I will often selectively add drops
of more concentrated acid to give
subtle variations across the glass.

That's when I start to paint on it. I'll
start painting using large brushes and quite
wet pigment. I put the pigment on and let it dry,

technique

Mary Mackey

and then blacken certain areas if I want the pigment to move a bit more. Then I let it dry and work into it with a badger brush or a smaller brush, emphasizing the movement taken by the wet pigment. Quite often, I leave it at that.

At other times, the panel requires a second working, so that the whole thing becomes layered; there will be a layer of the etching, a layer of the wet pigment and the dry one, and perhaps even a second firing. I often can't tell you in advance what I want; I just know in the doing. That versatility is one of the great things about painting.

INDEPENDENT PANEL
. . . and Flow
Painted stained glass
7" x 15" (18 cm x 38 cm)

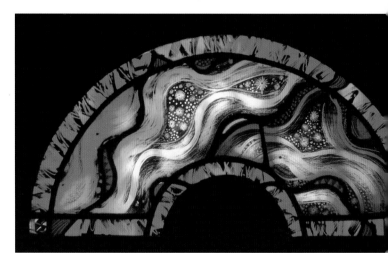

Mary Mackey

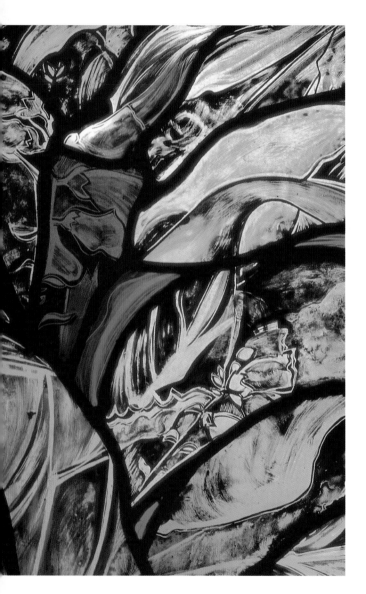

LIGHTBOX PANEL
Foxglove
Painted stained glass
15.5" x 12.5" (39 cm x 32 cm)

ENTRYWAY PANEL INSERTS
Moon over Minnane
Painted stained glass
2' x 3.5' (.6 m x 1.1 m)

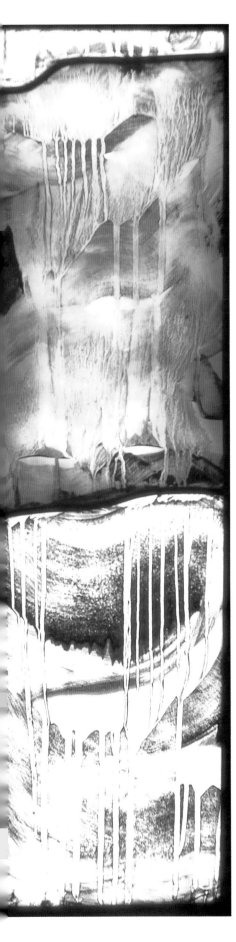

INDEPENDENT PANEL
In Contrast
Painted stained glass
16" x 13" (41 cm x 33 cm)

AUTONOMOUS PANEL FOR EXHIBITION
After Leenane
Painted stained glass
28" x 8" (71 cm x 20 cm)

FUSED GLASS
HOT HUES

Fusing represents an exciting and evolving addition to the glass

artist's repertoire, one that returns the glass to the heat from

which it was born. The process involves bonding one glass to

another with intense heat. An artist must master this highly

technical procedure to be able to translate a creative vision into

a finished piece. However, the results can be incredibly stunning:

shapes have dimension and definition, colors pop dramatically,

and the glass surface holds a remarkable luster.

Richard LaLonde has developed exceptional technical

refinements to create his wall-mounted murals. Once crafted, his

designs evoke the drama of the human connection to the natural

world, to spiritual and mystical dimensions, and to the past,

present, and future. Liz Mapelli also creates wall-mounted works,

ranging from mini-canvases of small fused tiles to larger pieces

that dominate the spaces they inhabit. Mapelli breaks with

convention to create abstract designs in hot-worked glass.

Brilliant colors and inviting textures characterize Maya Radoczy's fused and cast-glass artworks. She brings a fresh, exciting, and vibrant style to each new piece she creates. Judy Gorsuch Collins has also created a signature style, one that combines the playful with the practical. Her panels incorporate fused and traditional stained glass pieces to joyful effect. The result is a dynamic and fun-loving marriage of techniques that amplifies the best of both.

Judy Gorsuch Collins
INDIVIDUAL FUSED TILES, ST. ANNE'S SCHOOL
INSTALLATION (detail, right and opposite)
Tiles of stained glass fused on etched glass,
stained glass adjoining
4" x 4" (10 cm x 10 cm) each tile

It's no accident that Richard LaLonde found his creative voice in the kiln-fired milieu of fused

Richard LaLonde

glass—his artistic exploration began with heat. Using a welding torch, he began his career creating metal sculptures within the traditions of the craft movement of the early 1970s. LaLonde eventually found the medium stifling and went in search of greater color and artistic possibilities. That search ultimately led him to the growing culture of fused glass artistry.

Over the next two decades, LaLonde experimented, tested, and refined the process of fusing to serve his own artistic needs. Along the way, he pioneered techniques that were essential to creating his signature style.

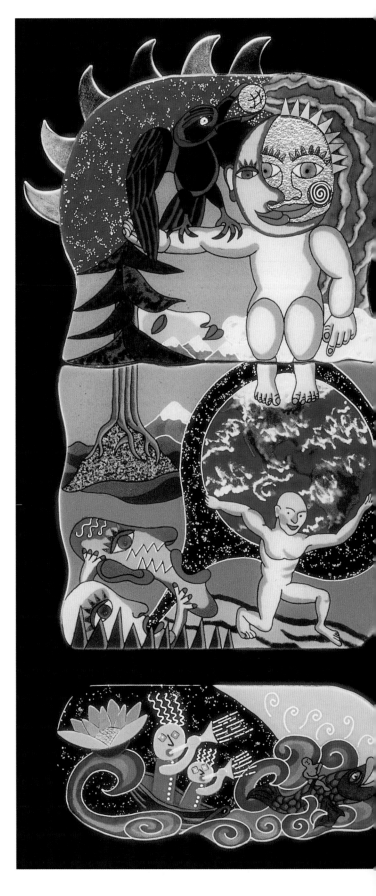

WALL MURAL
Mystic Messenger
Crushed colored glasses fused on clear glass
56" x 28" (142 cm x 71 cm)

His work is at once mysterious and obvious, a celebration of life in all its bright colors and an exploration of the mystery that lies beyond. These dualities echo throughout his pieces, in themes that juxtapose male and female, hard and soft, internal and external. He draws from a variety of cultures—from Native American to Guatemalan Indian—to create his own artistic mythology. And, just as LaLonde would have it, viewers can bring their own meanings and interpretations to this mythology and take away what means most to them.

WALL MURAL
Remember There Are Stars in the Sky
Crushed colored glasses fused on clear glass
52" x 76" (132 cm x 193 cm)

One of the biggest challenges I've encountered in fusing is actually crafting my large-scale mural work. Because kilns weren't available to do the size of work that I wanted to create, I built my own. Even so, my kiln is not large enough to fuse most of the murals in one piece.

To make a mural, I design sections to butt up against each other, creating the full design. After firing, I attach the fused sections onto aluminum backing plates with silicone adhesive, then use special picture-hanging hooks to hang the pieces. This way I can build murals as large as I want.

Another breakthrough was the use of crushed glass. Originally, I cut glass pieces and used them in much the same way you would in a stained glass window. But I wanted more freedom to use the color in a vibrant and fluid way, so I began using glass crushed to the consistency of table sugar. I pour it out in the design on the back of a piece of super clear glass (glass with no green tint to it). I then use a brush to "tone" up the line of the crushed glass. Finally, I tamp it down with a spoon, then fire the piece. This method has allowed for a lot of spontaneity, which adds to the unique character of my work.

WALL MURAL (left)
I Dream of Flying
Crushed, colored
glass fused onto
a clear sheet
54" x 66"
(137 cm x 168 cm)

Richard LaLonde

WALL MURAL (left)
Touch
Crushed, colored glass
fused onto a clear sheet
62" x 56" (157 cm x 142 cm)

WALL MURAL (right)
The Four Elements
Crushed, colored glass fused
onto a clear sheet
52" x 84" (132 cm x 213 cm)

WALL MURAL
The Hand of Humankind
Crushed, colored glass fused
onto a clear sheet
74" x 90" (188 cm x 229 cm)

WALL MURAL
World View
Crushed, colored glass fused
onto a clear sheet
43" x 66" (109 cm x 168 cm)

From the beginning of her career, Liz Mapelli has explored an unusual and dynamic new way

Liz
Mapelli

of utilizing glass. Her large-format commissions rely on the sense of depth inherent in the surface of fused glass. They are designed to be viewed in reflected rather than transmitted light, setting them apart from most other forms of stained glass art.

Mapelli's introduction to the technique of fused glass was as unusual as her style, through working in the front office of a pioneering glass company in Portland, Oregon. The company, Bullseye Glass, was the leader in the emerging arena of fused glass art, experimenting with techniques and compatible glasses. Mapelli was soon drawn to the unique and tactile qualities intrinsic to fused layers of glass.

She began by fusing small autonomous pieces, but broke through to create a larger

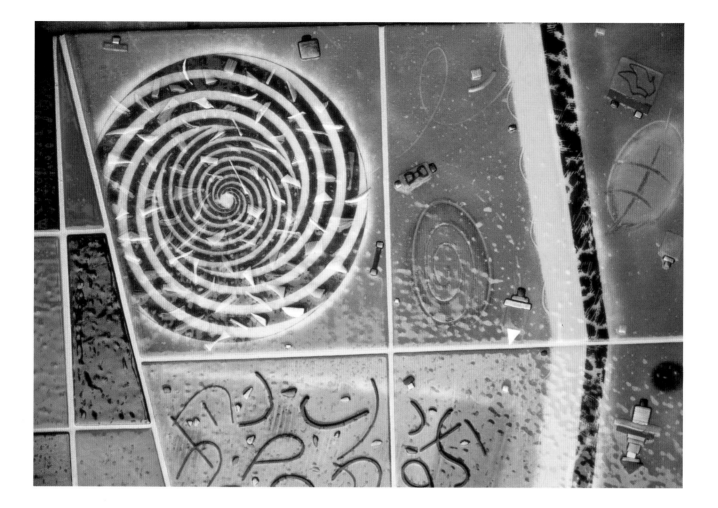

commission for the Portland Justice Center. From that starting point, she pursued large architectural commissions exclusively, projects that would allow her the range of expression she desired.

Impressive size is the first feature to attract attention to her work, drawing the viewer near. But upon closer inspection, Mapelli's fine detailing becomes apparent. Brilliant swirls, cubes, and chunks of vivid, shiny color seem to pop right off the surface. The magic of Mapelli's art resides in this transition from the large, unified design down to the amazing individual details that form the design.

WALL-MOUNTED TILES,
SUMNER ARTS CENTER (opposite and detail, above)
Fused and enameled stained glasses
30' x 4' (9.1 m x 1.2 m)

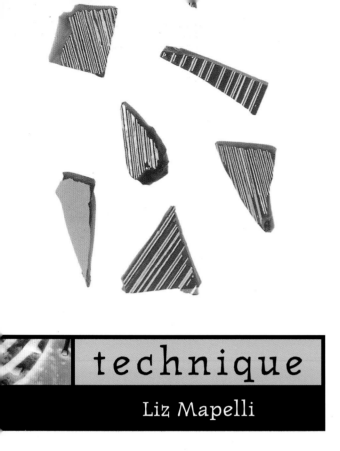

technique

Liz Mapelli

I work almost exclusively on large, architectural commissions. They bring with them many difficulties that have to be dealt with for the piece to remain intact and have lasting beauty. Many of these challenges relate to the details of the installation. A few years ago, I worked on a project to be installed in Colorado, where the climate was much less humid than where my studio is located in Oregon. I had glued the fired glass panels onto tempered Masonite, and when the piece got to Colorado, the glue shrank and all the glass broke. It was 6 feet by 42 feet (1.8 meters by 12.8 meters) of broken glass. I had to remake the entire project. Now, that's a learning experience.

To create large commissions, you need to have an organized, well-run studio. I work closely

with the architectural team on all projects. I work with a felt-tipped pen on transparent paper to develop a general concept. Then I start working with panels of glass testing out colors. From there, I lay out the piece full-scale and draw the imagery directly onto the glass. I start working enamels over the top, layering until I'm ready to start firing.

I think after fifteen years, I'm more realistic about the things I propose to do, but I still have a need to do new sorts of projects and try new techniques. Each project has its own, sometimes painful, learning curve.

WALL-MOUNTED SECTIONAL PIECES
Aloha Grotto
Fused and enameled stained glasses
9' x 11' (2.7 m x 3.4 m)

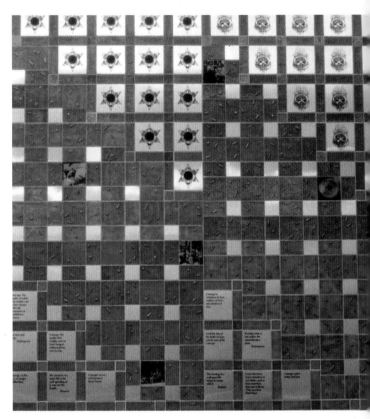

WALL MURAL (detail)
Memorial To Police And Fire
Fused and enameled stained glasses, stainless steel
14' x 16' (4.3 m x 4.9 m)

Liz Mapelli

WALL-MOUNTED SECTIONS
Galaxies—Peace Plaza
Fused and enameled stained glasses
25' x 4' (7.6 m x 1.2 m)

ONE IN A SERIES OF INDIVIDUAL
DECORATIVE TILES (detail)
Space Series Tile
Fused glass, enamels
8" x 8" (20 cm x 20 cm)

Bright and modern, Maya Radoczy's glass art represents a tour de force of fusing and casting.

Maya Radoczy

Her pieces are characteristically bright and playful, with stimulating colors set against a predominance of clear and textured glasses. Her work often incorporates textural elements, adding a sculptural dimension and maintaining the relationship of the glass to light.

Given her initial work in leaded glass, Radoczy's affinity for hot-glass techniques is somewhat surprising. After art school, she apprenticed at an eminent stained glass studio in Germany. There, she spent long, intense days studying painting, *dalle de verre*, restoration techniques, and other mainstays of leaded glasswork.

She might have stayed with leaded glass if she had not physically moved into the heart of

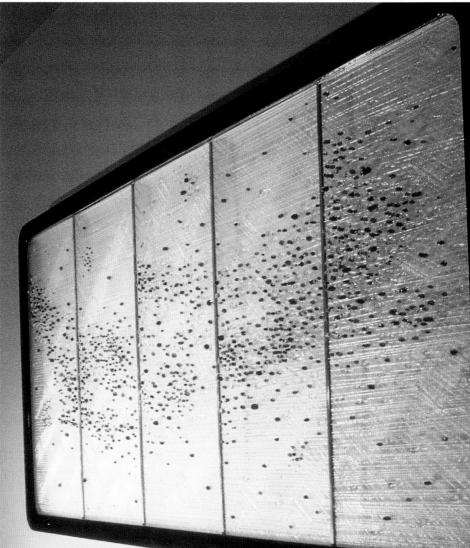

MOUNTED WALL SCULPTURE
(right and detail, opposite)
Fused glass
3' x 6' (.9 m x 1.8 m)

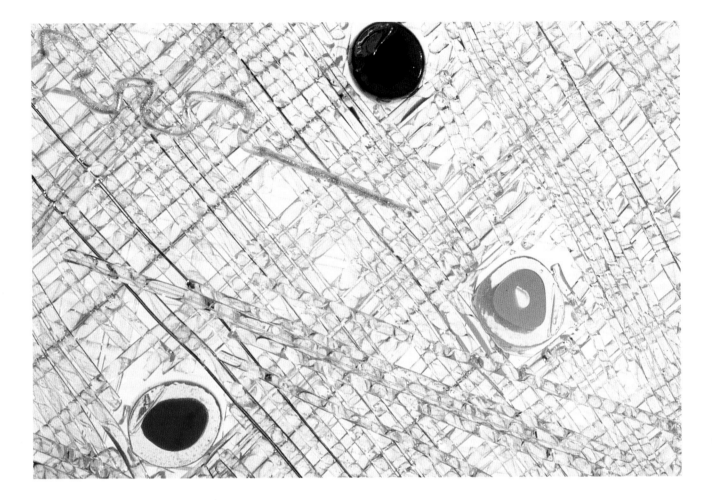

the emerging fused glass movement in Seattle, Washington. It may be that fusing—spontaneous, active, energetic, and charismatic—matched her artistic style.

Drawing from a platform of balance and clarity, Radoczy's work builds with a force akin to disparate atoms spinning as a unified whole. Her designs are formed from the combination of structures, making the finished pieces fascinating both from afar and up close. Radoczy's art inhabits a cheerful, lively galaxy that is as rewarding to the spirit as it is to the eye.

The excitement of fusing for me is the immediacy, the direct contact with the material. I feel I am a part of the studio glass movement, a modern development in which the glass artist works in a private studio rather than in a large factory system. In the factory system, the artist would give a design idea to craftspeople, who would then execute it. In the private studio, thanks to recent technical advances in miniaturization of furnaces and kilns, the artist can innovate by dint of working with the glass itself. This means that ideas are

technique
Maya Radoczy

not only coming from the sketch pad, but from the very process of working with the material.

I started fusing as soon as I moved to Seattle. I learned to blow, cast, and fuse glass. I sometimes use a combination of these to create an artwork. For example, I will take glass of a certain color and pull it into a rod. Then I will take the rod and put it onto another piece of glass, fuse them, cut them, and wind up with a varied, textured piece of glass. By combining techniques in this way, I can be quite painterly with the material.

DOOR PANELS,
REI LANDMARK BUILDING
24 hand-cast panels
11" x 17" (28 cm x 43 cm) each

Maya Radoczy

DOOR PANELS, REI LANDMARK BUILDING
(detail showing single panel with glacier image)

GLASS SCREEN FOR WINDOW
Fused and leaded handblown glasses
3.6' x 6.5' (1.1 m x 2 m)

MOBILE, CLERESTORY TOWER IN SCHOOL LIBRARY
Cast glass and metal tubing
3' x 6' (.9 m x 1.8 m)

Judy Gorsuch Collins first became aware of the power of stained glass while living in an older

Judy Gorsuch Collins

house in Colorado with a traditional stained glass window that enchanted her. But in her artistic explorations, the less-traditional technique of fusing held the most fascination. Her graphic design background had found a new means of expression, one that seemed perpetually fresh.

She most often articulates that expression in complicated architectural commissions that combine aesthetic requirements with a strong emotional or personal element. Typical is the Denver's Children's Museum glass wall. Built for hearing- and sight-impaired children, the glass

wall includes colored, clear, and textured glasses, unusual optical effects, and even metal disc knock-knock jokes in Braille. This playful, dynamic design embodies the tactile sense that forms so much of the attraction of art glass— the panels are meant to be touched as much as viewed.

Each of Collins's commissions possesses this sensitivity to the audience. She creates designs with color and texture that are appropriate to the space, but that also meet the more individualized ephemeral and cerebral needs of those who interact with the artwork. What remains constant for Collins, however, is her desire that the experience of the art, both in its creation and in its viewing, be rewarding for artist and audience alike.

GLASS WALL, DENVER CHILDREN'S MUSEUM
(opposite and detail, right)
Fused clear and stained glasses, machine glass, painting, sandblasting
8' x 20' (2.4 m x 6.1 m)

technique

Judy Gorsuch Collins

I really enjoy problem-solving, which is a constant in my commissions. I look to challenge myself with each commission, because I want to do something new and different every time. You can be incredibly accurate technically, using compatible glasses and annealing to scientific precision, but you will still be surprised sometimes. There are always variables, and the trick is to use them to your advantage.

I discovered this through experience, when I fired a sheet of double-rolled glass onto a sheet of single-rolled. Air bubbles were trapped, which would usually be an unpleasant surprise. But I have recently incorporated this unique effect in a commission to achieve an original and pleasing look.

In fact, it is no longer the errors in glass I worry about. At this point, I am confident of my skill in getting the glass to do what I want. I use a custom-built kiln and a computerized controller, so it is rare that things go wrong. It is in new materials that I'm looking for mystery and excitement.

My most recent explorations involve using metal as a partner to the fused glass. I have been layering metals between glass sheets and firing. I've found that one time the metal will do one thing and another time it will do something entirely different. Wherever this new work takes me, I'm fairly certain that new surprises are right around the corner.

COFFEE TABLE
Fused glass
4' x 2.5' (1.2 m x .8 m)

Judy Gorsuch Collins

WALL MURAL, CORPORATE OFFICE (detail)
Fused clear and colored glasses, enamels
10' x 3' (3 m x .9 m)

INTERIOR GLASS WALL, RESTAURANT (detail)
Fused, laminated, stained, and clear glasses
5' x 40' (1.5 m x 12.2 m)

DOOR AND WINDOW, OFFICE ENTRYWAY
Enameled and laminated glasses
11' x 6' (3.4 m x 1.8 m)

WINDOW, OFFICE ENTRYWAY (detail)

TILED GYMNASIUM
BREEZEWAY AND ENTRYWAY,
ST. ANNE'S EPISCOPAL SCHOOL
Fused glass tiles
240 square feet (21.6 square meters),
each tile 7" x 7" (18 cm x 18 cm)

ARTISTS' PROFILES
STAINED GLASS IN ARCHITECTURE

PROJECT: *Hope Valley Lutheran Church and Community Center*

CLIENT: *Lutheran Homes Incorporated*

SIZE: *Total area of project, 486 square feet (45 square meters)*

LOCATION: *Adelaide, South Australia, Australia*

ARCHITECT: *Matthews Architects, Adelaide*

One of two triptychs portraying the Baptism, the life of Jesus
Christ, and the Resurrection. Note the use of German handmade reamy, opal, and opak glasses and bevels.

Detail: Bright, antique glasses contrast with surrounding dense opak
screened and painted border, beveled crosses, and a ribbon representing
the Resurrection and promise of eternal life.

The second triptych is thematically related to music and the Miracle of
Pentecost. The screen-printed music on the left and the texts on the right offer a
visual link between the calligraphy in the sanctuary and the quilts at the rear.

Architectural Stained Glass Studio

312A Unley Road, Hyde Park 5061

Adelaide, South Australia, Australia

61 8 8272 3392 phone • 61 8 8272 3392 fax

Berin Behn and Jan Aspinall

Jan Aspinall and Berin Behn are South Australian-based glass artists who have collaborated in a quest to expand the horizons of contemporary stained glass and to promote its many applications in architecture. They are keen to create among architects and interior designers an awareness of the potential for incorporating glassworks in the early design stages of a project. Along with windows and doors, they have created glass for wall pieces, lift walls, screens, and office furniture.

When undertaking a project, many concerns and factors converge: the architectural concept, the function of the building, the requirements for color and light, the symbolic nature of the finished space, and any necessary heritage or appropriate historical associations or links.

Aspinall and Behn consider a significant part of their work is in achieving a balance of all these factors. Much of their combined efforts assure the glasswork harmonizes with its surroundings as an integral part of the framework of the building, yet retains a sense of artwork in itself.

Behn and Aspinall have more than twenty years combined experience and have won a number of awards, including the Royal Institute of Architects (South Australia) inaugural Art in Architecture Award in 1989, the inaugural Craft in Architecture Award of Merit (Crafts Council of South Australia and the RAIA), and an Art in Architecture Award of Merit and Commendation in 1993.

This interior overview features one side of the church from left to right, and highlights the sandblasted sanctuary windows, the dormer windows above the sanctuary, the center triptych windows, and the quilts along the back wall.

This detail of the midsection of the left-central column shows the various glasses and bevel.

Detail highlighting the contrast between cool grey opal and colored antique glasses.

PROJECT: *Adelaide Magistrates Court Redevelopment*

CLIENT: *Magistrates Court*

SIZE: *36 feet x 30 feet (11 meters x 9 meters)*

LOCATION: *Adelaide, South Australia, Australia*

ARCHITECT: *Denis Harrison, Building Project Management Services, S. A.*
Richard Brecknock, Brecknock Consulting

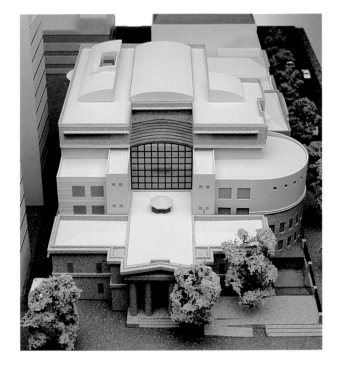

Model of project in progress. This is a major public redevelopment behind an existing historical building in the central square of Adelaide. Artwork is integrated throughout the building; the project is the gridded atrium window in the center of the photograph.

An exterior view of the window by night shows the texture of gray and clear reamy glass, clear rippled glass, and the colored, shaded borders and bands.

PROJECT: *ANZ Bank Redevelopment*

CLIENT: *Australian and New Zealand Banking Corporation*

SIZE: *33 feet x 8 feet (10 meters x 2.3 meters) plus 162 square feet (15 square meters) in same building*

LOCATION: *Gawler, South Australia, Australia*

ARCHITECT: *Swanbury Penglase Architects, Adelaide*

ARCHITECTURAL COMMISSIONS

Adelaide Magistrates Court
Adelaide, South Australia

ANZ bank
Gawler, South Australia

Beneficial Finance Corporation
Adelaide, South Australia

Centennial Park Cemetery Trust
Adelaide, South Australia

Church and Community Center
Lutheran Homes
Hope Valley, South Australia

Industrial Courts
Adelaide, South Australia

Our Lady of the Sacred Heart
Church and Community Center
Henley beach, South Australia

Strategic Management Services
Melbourne, Victoria

St. Andrew's Hospital
Adelaide, South Australia

Telstra Corporation
Adelaide, South Australia

AFFILIATIONS

Crafts Council of South Australia

Royal Institute of Architects, South Australia

A view of the "link" window from the alley. Its theme refers to natural and architectural bridges, hills, rivers, and building details, and it offers privacy from the alley.

PROJECT: *"Blue Dragon"*

CLIENT: *Reykjavik Art Museum, Reykjavik Municipal Theater*

SIZE: *6 feet x 25 feet x 1½ feet (1.8 meters x 7.5 meters x .5 meters)*

LOCATION: *Reykjavik, Iceland*

ARCHITECT: *Thorsteinn Gunnarsson, Olafur Sigurdsson, Gudmundur Kr. Gudmundsson*

A free-hanging stained glass kite designed to evoke joy and happiness. A combination of opal and opaque white glass and transparent glass offer a play of graphic textures and lines. The piece can be installed in different positions.

Stained Glass Artist

Laufasvegur 52

101 Reykjavik, Iceland

354 552 2352 phone • 354 552 2354 fax

Leifur *Breidfjord*

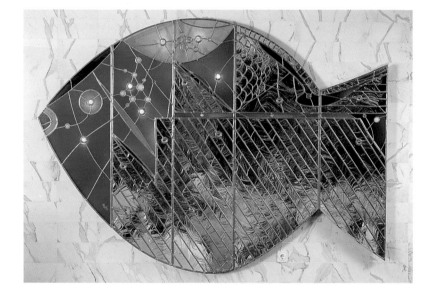

PROJECT: *"Silver from the Sea"*

CLIENT: *Engenerings Savings Bank*

SIZE: *6 feet x 9 feet (1.8 meters x 2.7 meters)*

LOCATION: *Reykjavik, Iceland*

ARCHITECT: *Johann Asmundsson*

The goldfish design features opal and transparent glass in conjunction with mirrored antique glass. The halogen light bulbs can be changed by taking away the prisms.

When creating an artwork of stained glass, four aspects of light have to be taken into account: Stained glasswork seen from inside the building during daylight, inside after dusk, outside the building in daylight, and outside in the evening.

Breidfjord already has a lifetime's worth of projects under his belt. His stained glass windows, both large and small, can be found in almost two dozen churches all over Iceland, as well as in churches in Germany and Scotland. St. Giles' in Edinburgh, the cathedral of Scottish Protestants, is perhaps the most famous example of his work. Another dozen of his windows grace banks, schools, and other public buildings in Iceland, including two architectural landmarks of recent origin: the National Library building and the newly inaugurated Supreme Court building. Recently, Breidfjord was commissioned to execute a stained glass window for a Reykjavik building of political rather than architectural consequence. The joint Anglo-German Embassy building is the only one of its kind in the world. Breidfjord also has provided his share of stained glass windows for private houses and collectors.

Two free-hanging stained glass kites designed to harmonize with the frame
structure of the architecture. Opal and opaque glass are used in contrast
with transparent glass.

PROJECT: *"Yearning for Flight"*

CLIENT: *Leifur Eriksson International Airport*

SIZE: *24 feet x 32 feet (7.2 meters x 9.7 meters) and
16 feet x 32 feet (4.8 meters x 9.7 meters)*

LOCATION: *Keflavik, Iceland*

ARCHITECT: *Gardar Halldorsson*

PROJECT: *"The Human Spirit: Past—Present—Future"*

CLIENT: *National and University Library of Iceland*

SIZE: *7¼ feet x 20½ feet (2.2 meters x 6.2 meters)*

LOCATION: *Reykjavik, Iceland*

ARCHITECT: *Mannfred Vilhjalmsson*

This work depicts three heads. The one on the left represents the
past, with text from old Icelandic manuscripts. The center one
shows the present, with text under a computer sign. The one on
the right shows the future, an unwritten sheet.

PROJECT: *"Flags"*

CLIENT: *British Embassy and German Embassy*

SIZE: *6 feet x 16 feet (1.8 meters x 4.8 meters)*

LOCATION: *Reykjavik, Iceland*

ARCHITECT: *Olafur Sigudsson*

The outside view of this window is as important as the inside view. The window is made of mostly opaque glass and opal-opaque white glass shading into clear glass. It shows free interpretation of the British flag on one side, with the German flag on the other. The Icelandic flag ties them together. The yellow stars from the European flag are scattered liberally throughout.

PROJECT: *"Med Logum Skal Land Byggja"*

CLIENT: *Supreme Court of Iceland*

SIZE: *5¼ feet x 32 feet (1.6 meters x 9.6 meters)*

LOCATION: *Reykjavik, Iceland*

A commission of stained glass for the Supreme Court of Iceland to harmonize with the curved lines of the architecture of the building. An experiment with bending a stained glass art work to achieve sculptural effects. The text is an old law text featuring Breidfjord's own calligraphy.

ARCHITECTURAL COMMISSIONS

British Embassy, German Embassy
Reykjavik, Iceland
Architect: Olafur Sigursson

City Hall
Eruption Memorial Window
Vestmannaeyjar, Iceland
Architect: Gudjón Samúelsson

Fossvogschapel
Reykjavik, Iceland
Architect: Olafur Sigurdsson

Grensáschurch
Reykjavik, Iceland
Architect: Jósep Reynis

Katholische Kirche
Steibis, Germany

Leifur Eriksson International Airport
Keflavik, Iceland
Architect: Gardar Halldórsson

National Bank of Iceland
Neskaupstadur, Iceland
Architect: Hróbjartur Hróbjatrson

P. Bröste A/S
Copenhagen, Denmark

St. Giles' Cathedral
Robert Burns Memorial Window
Edinburgh, Scotland, U.K.
Architect: James Simpson

Supreme Court
Reykjavik, Iceland
Architects: Margrét Hardardóttir,
Steve Christer

AFFILIATIONS

Félagi í Félagi íslenskra myndlistarmmanna
Félagi í Sambandi íslenskra myndlistarmanna
Félagi í British Master Glasspainters Society

PROJECT: *The Victoria Quarter*

CLIENT: *Prudential Assurance*

SIZE: *8,000 square feet (743 square meters)*

LOCATION: *Leeds, England*

ARCHITECT FOR RENOVATION: *Derek Latham & Company*

Brian Clarke was asked to contribute a proposal for a stained glass artwork to accompany the renovation of Queen Victoria Street in the center of Leeds, a street designed by theater architect Sir Frank Matcham and built in the nineteenth century.

In collaboration with renovation architects Derek Latham & Company, Clarke designed and fabricated a 400-foot-long (120-meter-long) colored rooflight that spans the existing street from end to end. The composition is the largest single work of stained glass in Great Britain. To allow plenty of natural daylight into the street and to reduce the amount of colored light falling on the already polychromatic tiling of Matcham's architecture, clear glazing was inserted where the eaves of the modern roof meet the Edwardian street facade. Visitors to the Victoria Quarter are treated to an unforgettable colored sky, which even on grey autumn afternoons, enlivens the space.

Toni Shafrazi Gallery

119 Wooster Street

New York, New York 10012

212 274 9300 phone • 212 334 9499 fax

TSGallery@aol.com e-mail

Brian Clarke

English-born artist Brian Clarke is acknowledged as one of the world leaders in architectural art. And although glass art is his primary artistic forum, he has not restricted his creative output solely to architectural commissions. His paintings, stained glass, mosaic, and tapestry works can be found in both architectural settings and private and public collections throughout the world.

His largest project to date, a recently completed shopping center in Rio de Janeiro, is illustrated here together with a smaller, though equally startling installation in southern Italy.

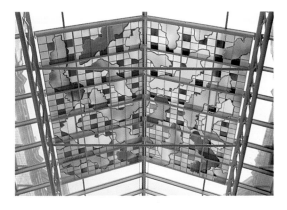

Clarke's previously completed architectural works include collaborations with architects Sir Norman Foster, Will Alsop, Arata Isozaki, Future Systems, Zaha Hadid, and Skidmore, Owings, and Merrill. In these commissions, he has displayed an unparalleled understanding and sensitivity toward the built environment and its integration with art.

Clarke executed the world's largest stage sets for the 1993 Paul McCartney New World Tour. Additional clients have included Pfizer Pharmaceuticals, the Swiss Bank Corporation, and the Abbaye de la Fille Dieu in Romont, Switzerland. In his art, Clarke expresses an insatiable appetite to collaborate at the highest level.

Clarke is a visiting professor of Architectural Art at University College London and an Honorary Fellow of the Royal Institute of British Architects. His work is represented by the Tony Shafrazi Gallery in New York.

PROJECT: *Norte Shopping Center*

CLIENT: *Engenharia, Comercio e Industria S.A.*

SIZE: *Stained glass: 11,356 square feet (1,055 square meters); mosaic: 1,572 square feet (146 square meters)*

LOCATION: *Rio de Janeiro, Brazil*

ARCHITECT: *Luis Carlos Pereira de Azevedo, Lindi, Brazil*

(top left)
The grand court of the Norte Shopping center is the focal point of the entire complex. A ring of mosaic interacts with the central stained glass skylight. The motif of ribbons uses bits of text, the words of which borrow from colloquial expressions of Carnival. The ribbon weaves and twists into both the mosaic and the stained glass.

(top right)
The stained glass and mosaic of the grand court as viewed from directly below.

(bottom left)
Another view down the principal mall showing the rooflight.

In this design, pools of light fall onto the floor of the conference theater and mute the inside room. The glass acts as a screen to the strong Mediterranean sunlight, and by virtue of the light coming through the glass, the room is animated by fragments of color.

At night, illuminated from within, the window forms a curved, radiant, colored frieze.

PROJECT: *"Espiral"*

CLIENT: *Private Residence, "Casa Malintzin"*

SIZE: *18 feet (5.5 meters)*

LOCATION: *Mexico City, Mexico*

ARCHITECT: *Eduardo Dyer*

Twenty-four panels, suspended from steel cables at different angles, form a helicoidal spiral, bathing a patio with bright, colored, and slowly moving images.

(opposite page)

PROJECT: *"El Vidrio en el Espacio y en el Tiempo"*

CLIENT: *Sílices de Veracruz, S.A. de C.V.*

SIZE: *10 feet x 10 feet x 10 feet x 36 feet (3 meters x 3 meters x 3 meters x 11 meters)*

LOCATION: *Orizaba, Veracruz, Mexico*

ARCHITECT: *Corporación Bajel, S.A. de C.V.*

STAINLESS STEEL STRUCTURE: *Servi-Estructuras Alfa, S.A. de C.V.*

Morelia Glass Design Center

Apartado Postal No. 670

58000 Morelia

Michoacàn, Mexico

52 4 323 1280 phone • 52 4 323 1280 fax

Bert *Glauner*

From his early youth, Bert Glauner's interests lay in art—or whatever looked like it. Against his family's stern resistance, he studied painting, jewelry design, and sculpture. Only vehement pressure from his father persuaded him to enter the family business and run a jewelry company. After long years in an industrial environment, he was introduced to glass artistry by a good friend from Boston.

Glauner feels that a strong, aesthetic design concept forms the basis for successful work in the field. He sees his creations as an integral part of the tectonic space; a symbiosis between space and light, enhanced and modulated by glass.

After all these years of playing with leaded stained glass he has experimented with new techniques of lamination and chemical bonding, opening up a whole new language of expression. Above all, what concerns him, and what he seeks to explore through his work, is the magical, the mysterious, and the sensual.

To commemorate the inauguration of a new furnace, this leading manufacturer of glass containers commissioned the artist to design and fabricate an allusive monument to glass.

PROJECT: *Glass mural for Board of Directors room*

CLIENT: *Banca Serfin, S.A.*

SIZE: *23 feet x 7¹/₄ feet (7 meters x 2.2 meters)*

LOCATION: *Mexico City, Mexico*

ARCHITECT: *Estudio J. Lóyzaga, S.A. de C.V., Edmundo Pérez Toledo*

Framed by a stainless steel structure, ten panels form a glass mural of laminated safety and mouth-blown antique glass, bevels, and sand carving.

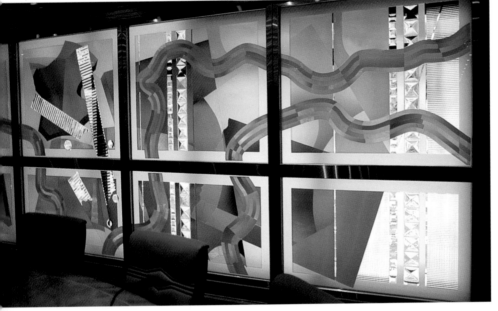

The half-view of the glass mural features sunlit bevels, accentuating shades of gray and blue patches of opal antique glass.

PROJECT: *Room divider*

CLIENT: *Estafeta Mexicana, S.A. de C.V.*

SIZE: *20 feet x 7¹/₄ feet (6 meters x 2.2 meters)*

LOCATION: *Cuernavaca, Morelos, Mexico*

ARCHITECT: *Eduardo Dyer*

Six laminated panels divide the director's office from reception area. The divider is constructed with sandwiched handmade bark paper, and is supported by a roughly polished steel structure.

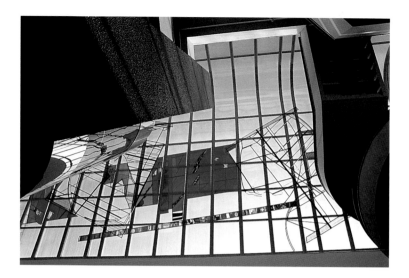

PROJECT: *Installation for polycarbonate-covered patio roof*

SIZE: *63 feet x 30 feet (19 meters x 9 meters), hanging at 45-degree angle under roof*

LOCATION: *Morelia, Michoacán, Mexico*

ARCHITECT: *Fernando Pérez Córdoba*

"Enigmas del Sacbé Perdido" is framed by an elevator shaft and sculpted staircase.

PROJECT: *Window for staircase*

CLIENT: *Banca Serfin, S.A.*

SIZE: *4¹⁄₄ feet x 12¹⁄₂ feet (1.4 meters x 3.8 meters)*

LOCATION: *Mérida, Yucatán, Mexico*

ARCHITECTS: *Ernesto Nataren, Pablo Caso, Agustín Paulino, Mauricio Mendoza, and Antonio Mondragón*

A design for the restoration of a beautiful turn-of-the-century mansion. The idea here is the juxtaposition of different styles; an original venetian-crystal chandelier hangs in front of the window.

ARCHITECTURAL COMMISSIONS

"Caminos de Michoacán"
Zirahuén, Michoacán, Mexico

Grupo Cail
Mexico City, Mexico

Hotel San Cayetano
Zitácuaro, Michoacán, Mexico

Houseboat, Harry D. Page
Sausalito, California

Residencia Grimm
Tepoztlán, Morelos, Mexico

Residencia Sada González
Mexico City, Mexico

Residencia Such
Mexico City, Mexico

Residencia Ugarte
San Sebastián, Spain

Templo El Corazón de María
Morelia, Michoacán, Mexico

Torre Acuario
Mexico City, Mexico

AFFILIATIONS

Asociación de Artistas Vidrio, A.C. (AAV, founding member)
Mexico City, Mexico

PROJECT: *Westminster Abbey Poets Corner*

CLIENT: *Westminster Abbey*

SIZE: *324 square feet (30 square meters)*

LOCATION: *London, England, U.K.*

ARCHITECT: *Christopher Wren*

Poets' Corner is one of the most visited sites in England. This memorial to the poets of Great Britain is a modern response to a historical setting. The window is built in the traditional style.

(opposite page)
This detail shows the complexity of technique: triple etching, three applications of paint, and plating of glass. Only through this uncompromising process can the emotion of glass color be achieved.

58 First Avenue

London SW14 8SR England, U.K.

44 181 876 6930 phone • 44 181 876 6930 fax

Graham *Jones*

Graham Jones, for many years predicted as the leading exponent in the younger generation of this medium, has now achieved an international reputation with a list of some thirty major commissions.

His work spans the architectural divide from medieval Westminster Abbey to the Far Eastern Tower in Shanghai, China of Lucky Target Square. Yet throughout this variety of work, Jones constantly strives for the original response that each commission should elicit. This, he believes, is the great challenge of architectural art.

Although early in his career Jones was acknowledged as a gifted colorist, his work can swing, if dictated by the building, to the purist transparency and

white of suspended flat glass walls. Such is the case in his 864-square-foot (80-square-meter), three-story entrance screen for Smith Klein Beecham Headquarters in Harlow, England. Here a cloud vortex in painted washes of etched glass is interspersed with minimal stripes of color, the drama strong but not overwhelming.

The challenge of the Westminster Abbey commission became a personal crusade for Jones. Contemporary art can inhabit any setting; here, the easy option would have been a non-statement or an egotistical, uncompromising slight on the historical setting. Jones, however, chose a strong, richly colored approach, taking quotations of style from the period to ease the transition into the Abbey's milieu. The result has been applauded by the critics.

His love of glass and his insistence that art must not be dictated by the medium has led him to push the boundaries of convention with the great glass workshops of Europe. Yet beneath all the technical processes in Jones' work lies the soul of an emotive painter.

PROJECT: *Minster Court*

CLIENT: *Prudential Properties*

SIZE: *5 feet (1.5 meters)*

LOCATION: *London, England, U.K.*

ARCHITECT: *G.M.W. Partnership*

This suspended glass sculpture adds drama to the main entrance of a London trading center.

PROJECT: *Stockport Shopping Mall*

CLIENT: *Hamerson Group*

SIZE: *600 square feet (180 square meters)*

LOCATION: *Stockport, England, U.K.*

ARCHITECT: *BDP Manchester*

This series of eighteen windows is a progression of color balance for both sides of a shopping arcade. A laminated glass process gives a collage effect.

PROJECT: *Main entrance screen*

CLIENT: *Smith Klein Beecham Headquarters*

SIZE: *864 square feet (80 square meters)*

LOCATION: *Harlow, England, U.K.*

ARCHITECT: *A.M.E.C. and the Hillier Group*

To screen meeting rooms from the main entrance lobby, sixty-three etched, tempered glass panels, laminated with pieces of antique glass, were suspended from yacht masts using a bolting system.

PROJECT: *Colmore Gate Office Complex*

CLIENT: *Church Commissioners England*

SIZE: *864 square feet (80 square meters)*

LOCATION: *Birmingham, England, U.K.*

ARCHITECT: *Seymore Harris*

This is the central section of a project that is wrapped around half of the ground floor of the entrance to the building. The main purpose of this abstract landscape is to semi-obscure the exterior walkway.

ARCHITECTURAL COMMISSIONS

Coca Cola Headquarters
London, England, U.K.

ICI Corporate Headquarters
London, England, U.K.

Lucky Target Square Hospital
Shanghai, China

Prudential Developments Office
Complex
Berkeley Square
London, England, U.K.

Shell Oil UK Ltd
ShellMex House
London, England, U.K.

Window triptych.

PROJECT: *St. Markus Church*

CLIENT: *Pastor Theodor Jordans*

LOCATION: *Bedburg, Germany*

ARCHITECT: *Trude Cornelius, Bonn, Germany*

Lower part of the angel window, 1965.

(opposite page)

PROJECT: *St. Adelheid, Geldern*

CLIENT: *Pastor Norbert Hoffacker*

LOCATION: *Geldern, Germany*

ARCHITECT: *Prof. Josef Ehren, Geldern-Veert, Germany*

Altar window, 1967, whose theme is the equality of human life. The circular graphic follows the design of a cross-section of a tree trunk.

Buchenweg 13

41334 Nettetal-Schaag, Germany

49 2153 70836 phone • 49 2153 70836 fax

Joachim *Klos*

Born in Weida/Thüringen, Germany, Joachim Klos studied at the state high school for architecture and fine arts in Weimar, where Professor Martin Domke was leading the foundation course in the meaning of Bauhaus. He continued his studies in Krefeld, in the department of stained glass and mosaic at the Technical Training College Niederrhein. One of his first commissions was the nave windows for the Gothic church in Mönchengladbach, Germany. In the forty years since then, Klos has been a stained glass designer, graphic designer, and color designer in the field of architecture.

Joachim Klos's work can be understood in the context of a Hugo Rahner treatise about the "playing human." According to Plato, the human being is a "living toy," not just a figure in the game, thrown around or put away by an unknown power and temper. He is built in a logistical way, an object of godlike artistic joy. And therefore, as Plato says, the best of him is to be playful: a human being who lightly, beautifully, and seriously in the fullness of confirmation, imitates the power of creation, as much as it is given to him.

PROJECT: *St. Martin Church, Veert*

CLIENT: *Pastor Josef Janssen*

LOCATION: *Veert near Geldern, Germany*

ARCHITECT: *Prof. Ehren, Geldern, Germany*

Addition of an octagon.

PROJECT: *Church Christ Our Peace, Duisburg*

CLIENT: *Pastor Günter Becker*

LOCATION: *Duisburg-Meiderich, Germany*

ARCHITECT: *Prof. Hannes Hermanns, Kleve, Germany*

Section of choir window.

ARCHITECTURAL COMMISSIONS

Christ Our Peace Church
Duisburg, Germany

Holy Ghost Church
Essen, Germany

Kreissparkasse
Schwäbisch-Gmünd, Germany

Police Academy
Hiltrup, Germany

St. Adelheid Church
Geldern, Germany

St. Antonius Church
Kevelar, Germany

St. Barnabas Church
Niedermormter, Germany

St. Markus Church
Bedburg, Germany

St. Martin Church
Veert, Germany

St. Nikolaus Church
Walbeck, Germany

Telekom Building
Osnabrück, Germany

PROJECT: *Police Academy, Hiltrup*

CLIENT: *The state of Nordrhein-Westfalen*

LOCATION: *Mübster-Hiltrup, Germany*

ARCHITECT: *Board of Works, Münster, Germany*

Glass front at the entrance hall.

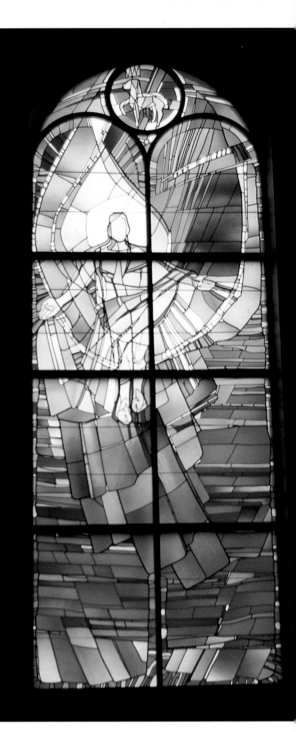

PROJECT: *Chapel window*

CLIENT: *St. Mary's Regional Health Center*

LOCATION: *Apple Valley, California*

ARCHITECT: *HBE Corporation, St. Louis, Missouri*

This window uses a woodcarved crucifix as the focal point.

PROJECT: *Resurrection window*

CLIENT: *St. Wendelin Catholic Church*

SIZE: *6 feet x 18 feet (1.8 meters x 5.5 meters)*

LOCATION: *Fostoria, Ohio*

ARCHITECT: *Dennis Mecham, Columbus, Ohio*

One of several leaded glass and sandblasted glass windows.

924 East Bethany Home Road

Phoenix, Arizona 85014

602 277 0167 phone • 602 277 0203 fax

Maureen *McGuire*

Maureen McGuire has walked a singular path throughout her life as an artist in stained glass. Childhood toys were supplemented or supplanted by those of her own making. Art training began early and few other occupations were ever seriously considered.

As an undergraduate student at Alfred University's New York State College of Ceramics during the "God is dead" era of the early 1960s, McGuire began creating designs in which He lived. Exercises in architecture became churches and chapels decorated by ceramic sculptures, woodcarvings in furniture designs, and graphic art. As the first design student allowed into what was until then the exclusive domain of the engineering school, McGuire began the first explorations in glass in a school now noted for its art glass program.

She continued her studies on scholarship at the Pope Pius XII Institute in Florence, Italy. There, she reinforced her connection to art history and symbolism and their importance in contemporary liturgical art. She worked in both stained glass and sculpture, receiving a Master's degree in 1964. The same year she accepted an offer to an apprentice position at the Glassart Studios in Scottsdale, Arizona. Honing her skills in all phases of the craft, she finally left Glassart's employ in 1968 to forge her own way as one of the United State's first independent stained glass designers.

Additional travel and studies with well-known German contemporary masters in architectural stained glass have strengthened Maureen's oeuvre. Following the demise of Glassart in 1987, McGuire established her own small studio to fill the gap left by Glassart and to satisfy her desire to better control some of her more innovative work. She continues to work with studios across the country principally, but not exclusively, in liturgically related commissions and still keeps active in sculpture and other forms of architectural art.

PROJECT: *Del Webb Corporate Center*

CLIENT: *Western Savings Company*

SIZE: *900 square feet (80 square meters)*

LOCATION: *Phoenix, Arizona*

ARCHITECT: *Cornoyer-Hedrick Associates, Pheonix, Arizona*

Leaded stained glass softens the light of the west facade and main entrance of a glass business mall structure.

PROJECT: *"The Conversion of St. Paul on the Road to Damascus"*

CLIENT: *St. Paul's Catholic Church*

SIZE: *500 square feet (44 square meters)*

LOCATION: *Phoenix, Arizona*

ARCHITECT: *Roberts-Jones Associates, Phoenix, Arizona*

Detail.

PROJECT: *Kitchen window*

CLIENT: *Bierny Residence*

SIZE: *9 feet x 9 feet (2.7 meters x 2.7 meters)*

LOCATION: *Tucson, Arizona*

FABRICATOR: *MMcGuire Design Associates, Phoenix, Arizona*

Leaded stained glass in a steel frame.

PROJECT: *Entry skylights*

CLIENT: *Lyon residence*

LOCATION: *Carefree, Arizona*

FABRICATOR: *Glassart Studio, Scottsdale, Arizona*

One of two clerestory windows to soften the east and west light in the living room.

ARCHITECTURAL COMMISSIONS

American Association of Retired Persons Corporate Headquarters Washington, D.C.

Arizona State University Sun Devil Stadium
Papal Visit Mass
Tempe, Arizona

Church of the Holy Eucharist Tabernacle, New Jersey

College View Seventh Day Adventist Church
Lincoln, Nebraska

Del E. Webb Corporate Center Phoenix, Arizona

First Christian/Disciples of Christ Church
Las Vegas, Nevada

Lakeview United Methodist Church Sun City, Arizona

Resurrection Mausoleum
St. Francis Cemetery
Phoenix, Arizona

St. Andrew Catholic Church
Cape Coral, Florida

St. Andrew the Apostle Catholic Church
Chandler, Arizona

St. Matthew's Baptist Church Louisville, Kentucky

St. Paul's Catholic Church Phoenix, Arizona

Woodlake Lutheran Church Minneapolis, Minnesota

AFFILIATIONS

Interfaith Forum on Religion Art & Architecture, a division of the American Institute of Architects

PROJECT: *Cherokee Memorial Mausoleum*

CLIENT: *Cherokee Memorial Park*

SIZE: *1,000 square feet (90 square meters)*

LOCATION: *Lodi, California*

ARCHITECT: *J. C. Milne, Portland, Oregon*

The leaded art glass in this interfaith mausoleum chapel was designed to the client's desire to uplift and glorify the human life cycle and to have recognizable colorful forms. The limited palette intensifies the impact of the primary color in each wall. The art glass was chosen to block a view of the dark stairs beyond, and to tie the work to the clear glass. Pulling colors from neighboring windows into the curving vertical forms and the background grids maintains the unity of the space.

Jean Myers Architectural Glass

11 Willotta Drive

Suisun, California 94585

707 864 3906 phone • 707 864 3467 fax

Jean *Myers*

Jean Myers has chosen to work in stained glass for two very personal reasons. First of all, the medium allows her to create art that enhances and enriches the experiences of human life. Myers designs work that becomes part of settings where people live out the most important moments of their lives—in homes, places of worship, places where people work and study, and places where people recover physically and spiritually. Her objective is to bring the warmth and beauty she sees in the world to these everyday settings.

Secondly, Myers works in stained glass because, as an artist, she finds the medium offers her the most direct link between personal vision and completed creation. Those elements that fascinate her as an artist—color, light, shape, form, and the gifts of the natural world—come to life most vividly, most passionately, in stained glass.

The tools of Myers's trade are not new. Artists have worked in stained glass for centuries. And although the world is a far different place than that reflected in the windows at Sainte-Chapelle, for instance, she feels a kinship with the people who created those jewels of vision. They were after some spiritual triumph, some evidence that the soul and spirit of mankind could prevail. Myers shares that vision, and through her art seeks to express her own celebration of all that is brilliant, beautiful, and optimistic in the world.

Myers's work in architectural glass contributes a voice that soars and sings in color and light.

PROJECT: *Hallway and conference rooms*

CLIENT: *Fuqua Industries, Inc.*

LOCATION: *Atlanta, Georgia*

ARCHITECT: *HDR, Omaha, Nebraska*

The client wanted to match the high-image profile of the building, while expressing the chairman's classic modern taste, using Georgian earth tones. In the corridor linking the executive spaces, the stepped walls are finished with stained glass panels that impart a sense of light and color to the interior spaces. Stained glass panels surround clear and pure white glass, adding a calm, airy mood as well as elegance to an unusually shaped boardroom.

PROJECT: *Mercy Hospital Chapel*

CLIENT: *Mercy Hospital*

LOCATION: *Folsom, California*

Myers's challenge was to create an uplifting work in a room with no windows. It also had to be able to withstand potential earthquakes. Her creation is suspended and sways gently from the slight breeze of the air conditioner. The work creates dancing visions of light and brings life to a space that otherwise could have been oppressive.

PROJECT: *Sanctuary Windows*

CLIENT: *Christ the King Catholic Community Church*

LOCATION: *Las Vegas, Nevada*

The client made three requests: That the windows contain content associated with the Triduum, that the imagery be expressed in new symbolism, and that they contain the colors of their desert environment. Myers's windows were found to be a successful solution to the exploration of the mysteries of death and resurrection.

ARCHITECTURAL COMMISSIONS

Cherokee Memorial Park
Mausoleum
Lodi, California
Architect: J. C. Milne

Christ the King Catholic Community
Church
Las Vegas, Nevada
Architect: G. C. Wallace

First Christian Church
Portland, Oregon
Architect: J. Pecsok

Fuqua Industries, Inc.
Executive Offices
Atlanta, Georgia
Architect: HDR

Geist Christian Church
Indianapolis, Indiana
Architect: McGuire/Shock

Mercy Hospital
Folsom, California
Architect: Anderson, DeBartolo &
Pan

Our Savior's United Methodist
Church
Schaumberg, Illinois
Architect: Richard Kalb

St. Ignatius Catholic Church
Antioch, California
Architect: Mossbacker

St. Mark's in the Valley Episcopal
Church
Los Olivos, California
Architect: R. Barrett

Zionsville Presbyterian Church
Zionsville, Indiana
Architect: J. Pecsok

AFFILIATIONS

American Institute of Architects

Stained Glass Association of America

Marin Society of Artists

American Craft Council

PROJECT: *St. Bernard Church, 1995*

LOCATION: *Hamburg, Germany*

Execution by Oidtmann Studio.

PROJECT: *Wiesbaden Town Hall, 1989*

CLIENT: *City of Wiesbaden*

LOCATION: *Wiesbaden, Germany*

Windows on a staircase. Execution by Derix, Taunusstein.

Theodor-Seipp-Strasse 118

52477 Alsdorf-Ofden, Germany

49 2404 1243 phone • 49 2404 24010 fax

Ludwig *Schaffrath*

Ludwig Schaffrath's career began in 1947 when he accepted a faculty position as a lecturer on free-hand drawing in the architecture department at the Rheinisch-Westfälische Technische Hoschule. In addition to lecturing at schools and universities in various countries including Japan, Australia, and the United Kingdom, in 1985 he became a professor at Staatliche Akademie der Bildenden Künste in Stuttgart, Germany.

PROJECT: *Private residence, 1982*

LOCATION: *Aachen-Rott, Germany*

Execution by Oidtmann Studio.

PROJECT: *Haus der kirchlichen Dienste*

LOCATION: *Friedrichshafen, Germany*

Glass wall.

PROJECT: *St. Leonhard Church, 1993*

LOCATION: *Frankfurt, Germany*

Execution by Oidtmann Studio.

PROJECT: *St. Lioba College, 1993*

LOCATION: *Bad Nauheim, Germany*

Execution by Oidtmann Studio.

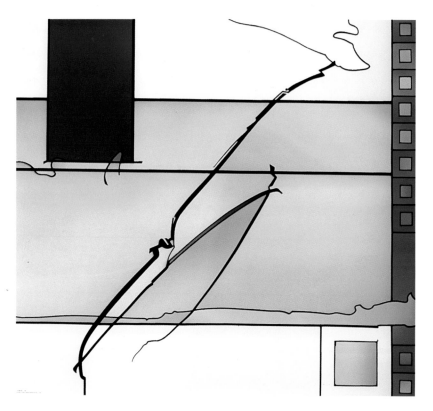

PROJECT: *Gallery house window*

CLIENT: *K. Kajiwara*

SIZE: *4¼ feet x 5 feet (1.3 meters x 1.5 meters)*

LOCATION: *Hita-City, Oita, Japan*

Window for the Kajiwara gallery house. Execution by Derix, Taunusstein.

(opposite page)

PROJECT: *Church window*

CLIENT: *Paulus Community*

SIZE: *9½ feet x 4½ feet (2.9 meters x 1.4 meters)*

LOCATION: *Rauenberg, Germany*

ATCHITECT: *Veit Ruser, Karlsruhe*

Window in the religious service hall. Execution by Derix, Taunusstein.

PROJECT: *Window for the election chapel, Frankfurt Cathedral*

CLIENT: *Bischöfliches Ordinariat, Limburg*

SIZE: *8¼ feet x 4½ feet (2.5 meters x 1.4 meters)*

LOCATION: *Frankfurt, Germany*

A grave divides a carpet of light from a carpet of darkness. A part of humanity lives in light and comfort but the majority live in suppressed darkness. At bottom left there is a reconciliation display. (The small chapel was the election place of kings and emperors of the Holy Roman Empire of the German Nation.) Execution by Derix, Taunusstein.

Rothkehlchenweg 7

63225 Langen, Germany

49 6103 71468 phone • 49 6103 71468 fax

Johannes *Schreiter*

Johannes Schreiter, born in 1930 in Annaberg-Buchholz/Erzgebirge, Germany, studied at the Westphalia Art School Münster, University of Mainz, and the Academy of Fine Arts, Berlin. In 1958 he won a scholarship to the Friedrich-Ebert-Stiftung, Bonn, where he invented his fire collage. From 1960 to 1963, he was director of the department *Fläche* in the School of Art in Bremen; in 1963 he moved to the Academy of Fine Arts, Frankfurt, where he was professor, head of the department of painting and graphics, and, from 1971 to 1974, president.

Since 1975, Johannes Schreiter has increasingly concerned himself with architectural art, primarily in the form of stained glass. He is best known outside of Germany for his work in window design, but his immense output in the field of graphics is also impressive.

Examples of his graphic work and window designs are collected in more than sixty international galleries and museums. Since 1960, he has completed many stained glass window commissions for churches and secular buildings. Awards include a gold medal in the Second International Biennale in Salzburg, 1960, an award at the exhibition "Contemporary European Graphic Art" in Salzburg 1974, and the Philip Morris prize for painting in 1977. In 1974 he received the BVK (the Cross of Merit of West Germany) and in 1984 the Medal of Honour at the second exhibition "Kleine Grafische Formen" in Lodz, Poland. He has lectured in Great Britain, the U.S., Canada, New Zealand, and Australia, with exhibitions in Europe, the U.S., Africa, Japan, New Zealand, Alaska, Brazil, India, and Russia.

PROJECT: *Window for St. Franziskus Church*

CLIENT: *Church Community*

SIZE: *20½ feet x 10 feet (6.2 meters x 3 meters)*

LOCATION: *Bad Kreuznach, Germany*

ARCHITECT: *Thomas Stahlheber*

Window dedicated to Klaus Eickhoff. Execution by Derix, Taunusstein.

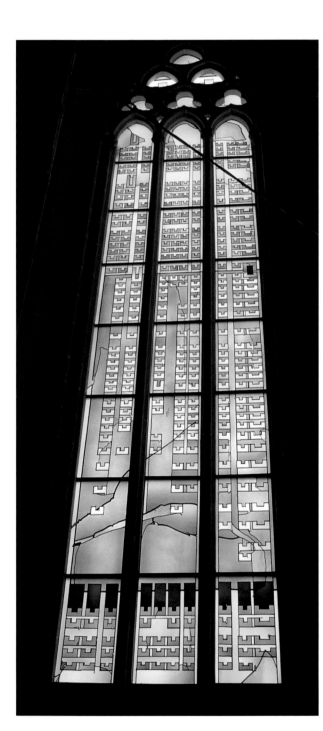

PROJECT: *Window for the Marktkirche*

CLIENT: *Church Community*

SIZE: *28¼ feet x 6¼ feet (8.6 meters x 1.9 meters)*

LOCATION: *Goslar, Germany*

Choir window located on the northeast side of the church. Execution by Derix, Taunusstein.

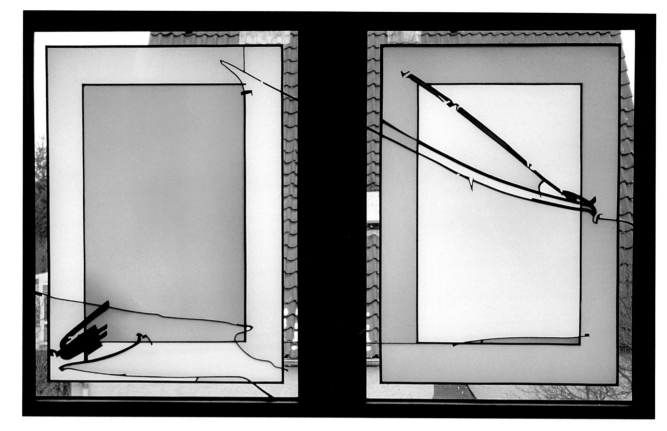

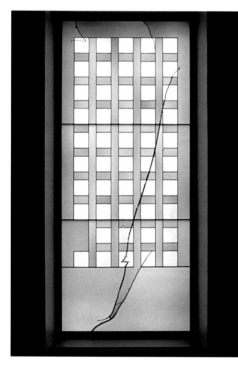

PROJECT: *Studio windows*

CLIENT: *Prof. Dr. J. Meyer*

SIZE: *3¹/₄ feet x 2³/₄ feet (1 meter x .8 meter) each*

LOCATION: *Bremerhaven, Germany*

What is visible through the imitation passepartouts is in a meditative colorfield context with a lead sketch: introduction for tension and release (G. Sehring). Execution by Derix, Taunusstein.

ARCHITECTURAL COMMISSIONS

Airport Chapel
Frankfurt, Germany

Christus Church
St. Ingert, Germany

Evangelical Church of Hessen and
Nassau
Darmstadt, Germany

Foreign Office
Bonn, Germany

Frankfurt Cathedral
Frankfurt, Germany

Grunewald Church
Berlin, Germany

Kajiwara Gallery
Hita-City, Japan

Reconciliation Church
Plauen, Germany

St. Franziskus Church
Bad Kreuznach, Germany

AFFILIATIONS

Deutscher Künstlerbund

Westdeutscher Künstlerbund

Neue Darmstädter Sezession

PROJECT: *Window for the Chancellery
Office Building*

CLIENT: *Evangelical Church of Hessen
and Nassau*

SIZE: *10 feet x 4 feet (3 meters x 1.2 meters)*

LOCATION: *Darmstadt, Germany*

Staircase windows. Execution by Derix, Taunusstein.

PATTERNS

All the projects in this book have an accompanying pattern. They are presented on the following pages. The percentage shown below each pattern indicates whether a pattern has been reduced or enlarged. If the pattern is not shown actual size, you'll need to enlarge or reduce accordingly to attain the correct size or the dimensions of the piece. However, with a photocopier, you can easily reduce or enlarge the pattern to suit your needs. See Preparing Patterns on page 10. Also, if a required pattern is a simple shape (such as a plain square with no ornamentation or added elements), we have only provided measurements for those patterns (for example, a 5" by 5" [13 cm by 13 cm] square that will act as the bottom of a candleholder). You'll need to measure and cut out the pattern on a sturdy piece of paper or thin cardboard (such as a manila folder).

Patterns are easy to design yourself once you learn the basics of stained glass assembly. Similar to a mosaic, pattern pieces must fit together like a puzzle. Once you get to know glass, you'll soon realize that soldering lines have to be placed in certain areas of a design out of necessity. Learn to use these restrictions in creative ways, adjusting your original design if needed. Remember, soldered seams are as much a part of the design as the shapes and colors of the glass.

You'll also quickly discover what kind of pieces are difficult to cut and which are easier. In the beginning, try to avoid the temptation to create difficult patterns that would be frustrating for a novice to construct; you'll only end up getting discouraged, though with some practice, you'll be able to make that window-sized landscape! Once you understand what makes a successful pattern, you'll be able to convert any image to glass, from photographs to paintings.

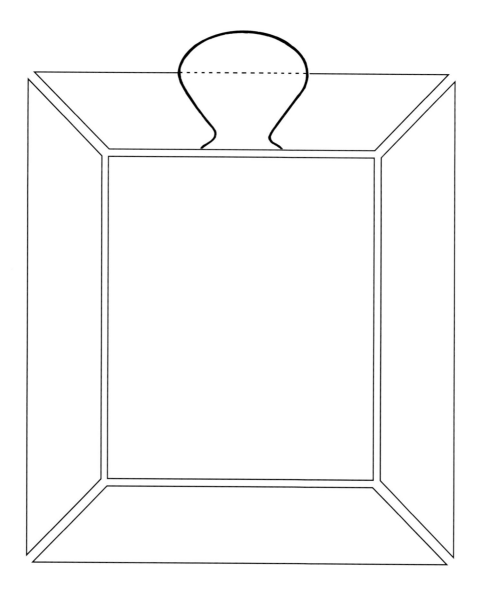

Mermaid Mirror, page 18
(shown at 50%)

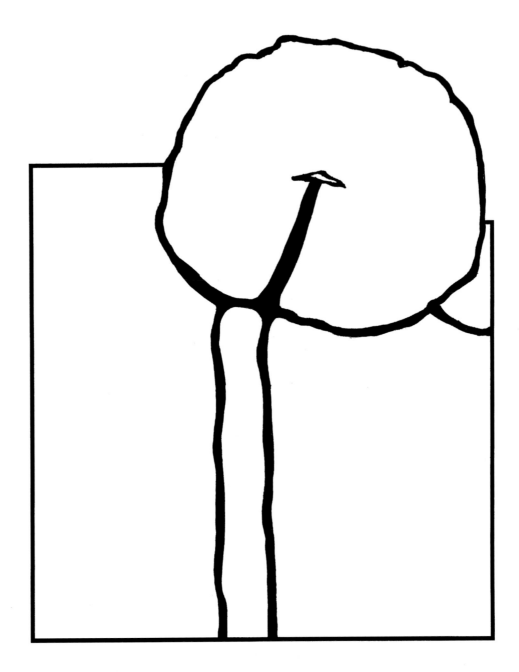

FRONT

SIDES/BOTTOM
Cut out three squares measuring 5" x 5" (13 cm x 13 cm) for the
two sides and the bottom.

Geode Candleholder, page 22
(shown at 100%)

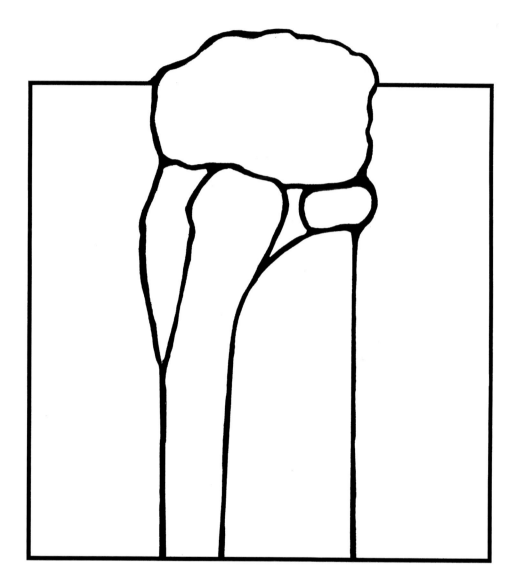

BACK

Trinket Tray, page 26
(shown at 100%)

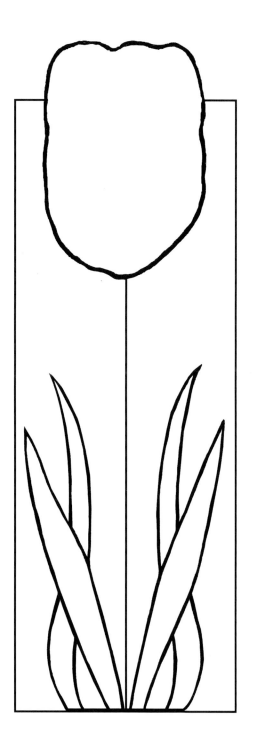

SIDES
Cut three 8" x 3" (20 cm x 8 cm) rectangles for the sides.

BOTTOM
Cut one 3" x 3" (8 cm x 8 cm) square for the bottom.

Tulip Vase, page 32
(shown at 80%)

FRONT/BACK

CUT 2

BOTTOM

Art Deco Napkin Holder, page 36
(shown at 100%)

Mooncatcher, page 40
(shown at 100%)

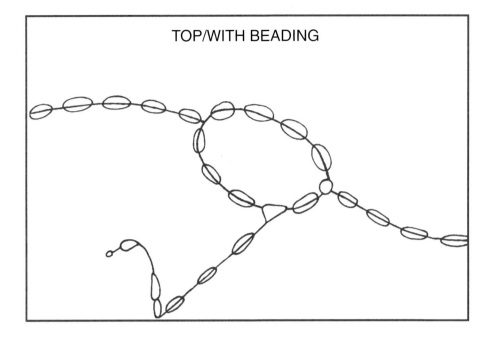

TOP/WITH BEADING

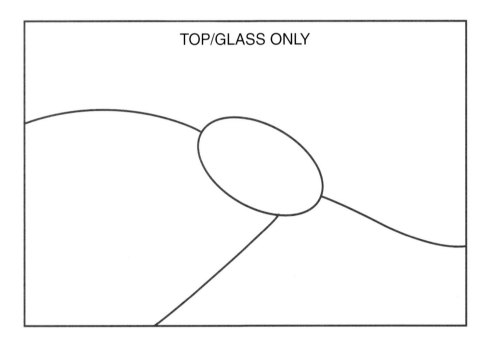

TOP/GLASS ONLY

FRONT AND BACK SIDES
Cut two 1¹/₂" x 6" (4 cm x 15 cm) rectangles for the front and back sides.

LEFT AND RIGHT SIDES
Cut two 1¹/₂" x 4" (4 cm x 10 cm) rectangles for the left and right sides.

BOTTOM
Cut two 4" x 5³/₄" (10 cm x 15 cm) rectangles for the bottom.

Cabochon Jewelry Box, page 46
(shown at 80%)

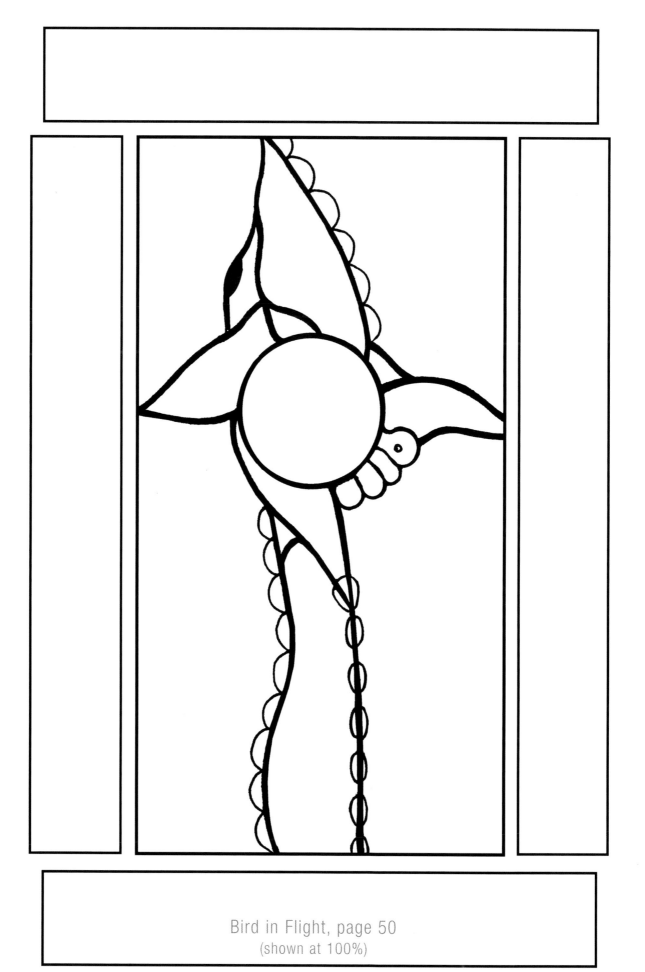

Bird in Flight, page 50
(shown at 100%)

FRONT

BOTTOM

BACK

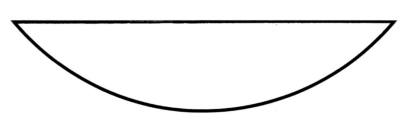

Tree Tea Light, page 54
(shown at 100%)

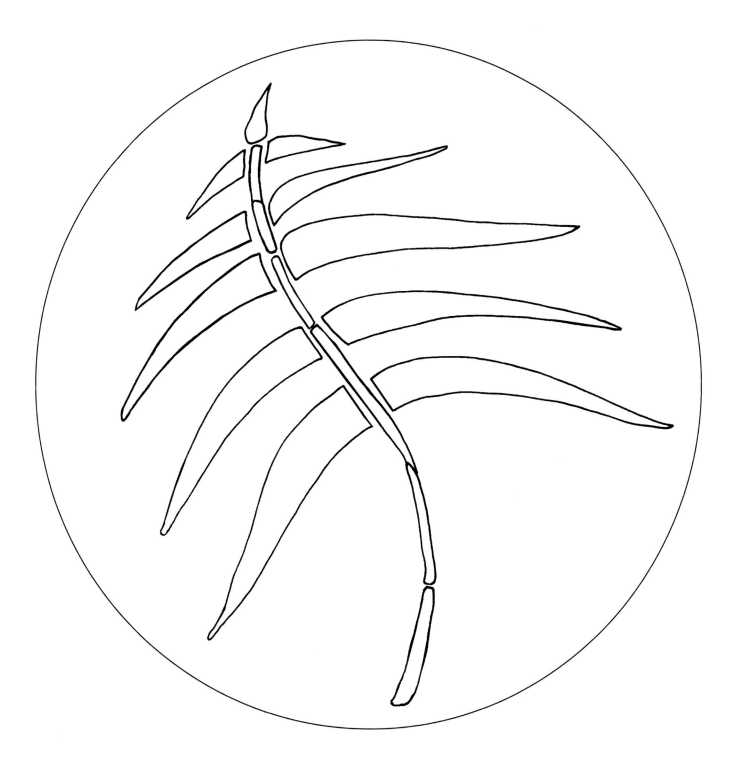

Fern Plate, page 68
(shown at 80%)

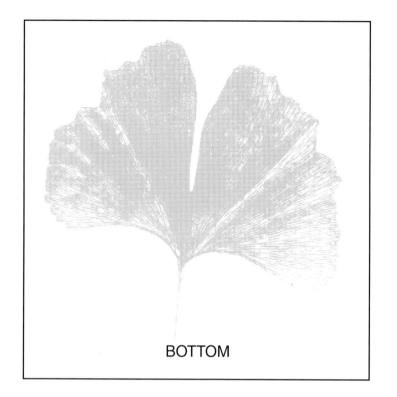

BOTTOM

TOP

Organic Tiles, page 72
(shown at 100%)

Art Glass Display Bowl, page 76
(shown at 100%)

Fluted Candlestick, page 80
(shown at 100%)

Resources

Albion Glass and Mirror
P.O. Box 27
Albion Q 4010, Australia
Phone: (61) 3862 6227
Fax: + (61) 3262 7605
E-mail: help@albionglass.com.au
Website: www.albionglass.com.au
Stained glass supplies; offers courses and workshops

B & B Etching Products
19721 N. 98th Avenue
Peoria, AZ 85382, USA
Phone: (888) 382-4255
Fax: (803) 584-7315
E-mail: etchall@etchall.com
Website: www.etchall.com
Etching crème and supplies; order custom adhesive
vinyl stencils from your sketches for a small fee

Centre DeVerre
18 Bartlett Street
Allenstown, NH 03275, USA
Phone: (800) 958-5319; (603) 485-8344
Fax: (603) 485-2444
E-mail: service@cdvkiln.com
Website: www.cdvkiln.com
Kilns and kiln accessories; glass paints

Delphi Stained Glass
3380 East Jolly Road
Lansing, MI 48910, USA
Phone: (800) 248-2048; (517) 394-4631
Fax: (800) 748-0374; (517) 394-5364
E-mail: sales@delphiglass.com
Website: www.delphiglass.com
Stained glass and fusing supplies

Fantasy In Glass
703 The Queensway
Toronto, ON M8Y 1L2, Canada
Phone: (416) 252-6868
Fax: (416) 252-8915
Toll-free: (800) 841-5758
Website: www.fantasyinglass.com
Stained glass supplies; some fusing supplies

The Glass Art Society (GAS)
1305 Fourth Avenue, Suite 711
Seattle, WA 98101, USA
Phone: (206) 382-1305
Fax: (206) 382-2630
E-mail: info@glassart.org
Website: www.glassart.org
The GAS is an international nonprofit organization
whose purpose is to encourage excellence, to advance
education, to promote the appreciation and development of the glass arts, and to support the worldwide
community of artists who work with glass. Membership
is open to anyone interested in glass art.

Glass Crafters Stained Glass, Inc.
398 Interstate Court
Sarasota, FL 34240, USA
Phone: Orders: (800) 422-4552
Customer Service: (941) 379-8333
Fax: (941) 379-8827
E-mail: info@glasscrafters.com
Website: www.glasscrafters.com
Stained glass and fusing supplies

Hee Sun Stained Glass, Inc.
324 Main Street
Reistertown, MD 21136, USA
Phone: (888) 508-5595; (410) 833-3007
E-mail: sales@heesun.com
Website: www.heesun.com/catalog.html
Stained glass supplies; some fusing supplies

HobbyCraft (stores throughout the UK)
Head Office
Bournemouth
Phone: 01202 596 100
Supplies glass paint and glass work tools

Hot Glass Horizons
15500 NE Kincaid Road
Newberg, OR 97132, USA
Phone: (503) 538-5281
Fax: (503) 538-6527
E-mail: glaswiz@aol.com
Website: www.hotglasshorizons.com
Fusing supplies

Hot Glass Supply
E-mail: sales@hotglasssupply.com
Website: www.hotglasssupply.com
Sells Spectrum System 96 for fusing and kilns

The International Guild of Glass Artists
1025 Yorkshire Road
Grosse Pointe Park, MI 48230, USA
Phone/Fax: (313) 886-0099
E-mail: igga@warmglass.com
Website: www.igga.org
IGGA is an international nonprofit association
of artists, artisans, and craftspeople who work
with glass.

James Hetley & Co. Ltd.
Glasshouse Fields, Stepney
London E1W 3JA, United Kingdom
Phone: (0)20 7790 2333
Fax: (0)20 7790 0201
Website: www.hetleys.co.uk
Stained glass supplies; some fusing supplies

Kansa Craft
The Old Flour Mill
Wath Road
Elsecar
Barnsley
S Yorks S74 8HW, United Kingdom
Phone: 01226 747 424

Lead & Light
The Old Flour Mill
35a Hartland Road
London NW1 4DB, United Kingdom
Phone: 0207 485 0997

Skutt Kilns
6441 S.E. Johnson Creek Boulevard
Portland, OR 97206, USA
Phone: (503) 774-6000
Fax: (503) 775-7833
E-mail: skutt@skutt.com
Website: www.skutt.com

Stained Glass Warehouse, Inc.
P.O. Box 609
Arden, NC 28704, USA
Phone: (828) 687-1057
Fax: (828) 684-8861
E-mail: info@stainedglasswarehouse.com
Website: www.stainedglasswarehouse.com
Stained glass and fusing supplies; kilns

Tempsford Stained Glass
The Old School
Tempsford
Sandy Beds, SG19 2AW, United Kingdom
Phone: + (44) 767 640 235
Website: www.tempsford.net
Suuplies store, showroom, and studio

www.craft-fair.co.uk
Online directory of craftmakers, craft fairs,
craft suppliers, and craft news

PERIODICALS

Glass Craftsman magazine
P.O. Box 678
Richboro, PA 18954, USA
Phone: (800) 786-8720; (215) 826-1799
Fax: (215) 826-1788
E-mail: custsvc@glasscraftsman.com
Website: www.glasscraftsman.com
A bi-monthly publication that features the
work of the world's top glass artists; offers
tips, techniques, workshop and even information
and book and video reviews.

Glass Patterns Quarterly
P.O. Box 69
Westport, KY 40077, USA
Phone: (800) 719-0769
Fax: (502) 222-4527
E-mail: gpqmag@aol.com
Website: www.glasspatterns.com
A quarterly publication that offers instruction
on glass etching, fusing, leading, copperfoil,
soldering, beveling, slumping, painting, overlay
techniques, and more.

Directory of Artists

Arte en Vidrio
Eng. Raul Urbina Torres,
Mrs. Leticia Martinez de Urbina,
and Mrs. Rosario Lopéz Balam
A.P. 88 Cordemex
Mérida, Yucatán 97310, Mexico
Phone: (999) 922 0081
E-mail: raulurbi@sureste.com
Website: www.arteenvidrio.com

Sigrídur Asgerisdóttir
Dràpuhlid 13
105 Reykavik, Iceland
Phone: (354) 551-1031

Berin Behn and Jan Aspinall
Architectural Stained Glass Studio
312A Unley Road, Hyde Park, 5061
Adelaide, South Australia, Australia
Phone/Fax: + (618) 8272 3392

Leifur Breidfjord
Stained Glass Artist
Laufasvegur 52
101 Reykavik, Iceland
Phone: (354) 552-2352
Fax: (354) 552-2354

Jessy Carrara
LightGarden Glass Art Studio
1086 Washburn
Medford, OR 97501, USA
Phone: (541) 799-0272
Website: www.lightgarden.com

Brian Clarke
Toni Shafrazi Gallery
119 Wooster Street
New York, NY 10012, USA
Phone: (212) 274-9300
Fax: (212) 334-9499
E-mail: TSGallery@aol.com

Judy Gorsuch Collins
8283 West Iliff Lane
Lakewood, CO 80227, USA
Phone: (303) 985-8081
Fax: (303) 980-0692

Debora Coombs
R.R. 1, Box 531
Reedsboro, VT 05350, USA
Phone/Fax: (802) 423-5869

Eduard Deubzer
Glashüttenweg 7
94258 Frauenau, Germany
Phone: + (49) 9926 90 20 85
Website: www.deubzer.de

Marie Pascale Foucault-Phipps
The Quarter Circle Bell Ranch
41348 Road 29
Elizabeth, CO 80107, USA
Phone: (303) 646-4784
Fax: (303) 646-4765

Bert Glauner
Morelia Glass Design Center
Apartado Postal No. 670
58000 Morelia
Michoacàn, Mexico
Phone/Fax: + (52) 4 323 1280

Lutz Haufschild
Gotthard Strasse 26
8800 Thalwil, Switzerland
Phone/Fax: + (41) 1722 11 38

Virginia Hoffman
P.O. Box 2712
Sarasota, FL 34230, USA
Phone: (941) 365-7450

Anja Isphording
829 18th Ave. W.
Vancouver, B.C. V5Z 1W2, Canada
E-mail: anjaisphording@yahoo.de
Website: www.pages.sprint.ca/
anjaisphording/ files/index.htm

Graham Jones
58 First Avenue
London SW14 8SR England,
United Kingdom
Phone/Fax: + (44) 181 876 6930

Shelley Jurs
4167 Wilshire Boulevard
Oakland, CA 94602, USA
Phone: (510) 521-7765
Fax: (510) 531-6173

Kuni Kajiwara
1996-1 Oturumachi
Hita-City, Oita-Ken, Japan
Phone: + (81) 973 28 2105
Fax: + (81) 973 28 2626

Joachim Klos
Buchenweg 13
41334 Nettetal-Schaag, Germany
Phone/Fax: + (49) 2153 70836

Richard LaLonde
4651 South Melody Lane
Freeland, WA 98249, USA
Phone: (360) 730-2166
Fax: (360) 730-2151

Rafael Navarro Leiton
Pura Vida Glass and Clay
P.O. Box 4
Point Roberts, WA 9828, USA
Phone: (604) 278-0864
Website: www.puravidaarts.com

Linda Lichtman
17 Tudor Street
Cambridge, MA 02139, USA
Phone: (617) 876-4660
Fax: (617) 354-1119

Mary Mackey
Coachman's House
Laurel Walk
Bandon, County Cork, Ireland
Phone: + (353) 23 44402

Ellen Mandelbaum
39-49 46th Street
Long Island City, NY 11104, USA
Phone/Fax: (718) 361-8154

Liz Mapelli
P.O. Box 3885
Portland, OR 97208, USA
Phone: (503) 796-0221

Maureen McGuire
924 East Bethany Home Road
Phoenix, AZ 85104, USA
Phone: (602) 277-0167
Fax: (602) 277-0203

Rick Melby
37 Biltmore Avenue
Asheville, NC 28801, USA
Phone: (704) 232-0905

Jean Myers
Jean Myers Architectural Glass
11 Willotta Drive
Suisun, CA 94585, USA
Phone: (707) 864-3906
Fax: (707) 864-3467

Carl Powell
1610 Ninth Street
Berkeley, CA 94710, USA
Phone: (510) 526-2637

Maya Radoczy
P.O. Box 31422
Seattle, WA 98103, USA
Phone: (206) 527-5022
Fax: (206) 524-9226

Patrick Reyntiens
Ilford Bridges Farm
Close Stocklinch
Ilminster, Somerset, United Kingdom
Phone: + (44) 1460 52241
Fax: + (44) 1460 57150

Ludwig Schaffrath
Theodor-Seipp-Strasse 118
52477 Alsdorf-Ofden, Germany
Phone: + (49) 2404 1243
Fax: + (49) 2404 24010

Andrea and Brian Scholes
Scholes Studios
149 Mason Stree
Fall River, MA 02723, USA
Phone: (508) 676-9165
Website: www.scholesstudios.com

Rachel Schutt-Mesrahi
50 Oak Knoll Avenue
San Anselmo, CA 95960, USA
Phone: (415) 454-8537
Fax: (415) 721-0607

Kenneth vonRoenn
1110 Baxter Avenue
Louisville, KY 40204, USA
Phone: (502) 585-5421
Fax: (502) 585-2808

David Wilson
202 Darby Road
South New Berlin, NY 13843, USA
Phone: (607) 334-3015

Larry Zgoda
2117 West Irving Park Road
Chicago, IL 60618, USA
Phone: (773) 463-3970
Fax: (773) 463-3978

For further information on the history and the art of stained glass, contact the following organizations:

The Corning Museum of Glass
One Museum Way
Corning, NY 14830, USA
Phone: (607) 937-5371
Fax: (607) 937-3352

The Stained Glass Association of America
P.O. Box 22642
Kansas City, MO 64113, USA
Phone: (800) 888-7422
Fax: (816) 361-9173

The Stained Glass Museum
10 Ferry Lane
Chesterton, Cambridge CB4 1NT, United Kingdom
Phone: + (44) 01223 327367
Fax: + (44) 01223 327367

Photography Credits

Bobbie Bush Photography
www.bobbiebush.com

Debora Coombs
Out of Confusion, Inner Room, Young Willows . . ., and *Woman* from the series "One Woman's Narrative," Collection Dr. Gordon Bowe, Dublin, Ireland.
Photos by Brian Nash

Lutz Haufschild
Spectra Veil Sample and *Blue Heart,* Fabricated by Wilhelm Derix Studios, Taunusstein, Germany
The Four Seasons, Glass, The Fire, Fighting Window, and *Time and Space*
Photos by Lutz Haufschild

Tribute to Baseball
Photo by Otto Bierwagen

Richard LaLonde
Mystic Messenger, World View, The Four Elements, I Dream of Flying, The Hand of Humankind, and *Touch*
All photos by Roger Schreiber

Kenneth vonRoenn
Doors, Glass Sculptural Column
Photos by Mike Robertson

Entryway
Photo by John Beckman/Quadrant Photography

David Wilson
Window, Nation's Bank
Dichroic Glass Doors (page 120) and Window (page 121, top)
Photos by Kevin Roche, John Dinkeloo & Associates, Architects

Creation Window, Beth David Congregation
Photo by Shapiro, Petrauskas, Gelber, Architects

Window (page 121, bottom)
Photo by Cass & Associates, Architects

Barrel Vault Window
St. Paul's Catholic Church
Photo by The Ashford Group, Architects

Berin Behn and Jan Aspinall
Hope Valley Lutheran Church and Community Center photos and Adelaide Magistrates Court Redevelopment detail **photos by Berin Behn**
Hope Valley Lutheran Church and Community Center interior overview **photo by Trevor Fox**
Adelaide Magistrates Court Redevelopment project model **photo by David Campbell**
ANZ Bank Redevelopment **photos by Bart Maiorana**

Leifur Briedfjord
"Blue Dragon" detail, "Silver from the Sea," "Yearning for Flight," "The Human Spirit: Past-Present-Future," "Flags," and "Med Logum Skal Land Byggja"
photos by Leifur Porsteinsson
"Blue Dragon" **photo by artist**

Brian Clarke
Photos by Stuart Blackwood, Richard Waite, Paul Warchol, and the Toni Shafrazi Gallery

Jean Myers
Cherokee Memorial Mausoleum **photos by Joel Simon**
Fuqua Industries detail, Christ the King Catholic Community Church, and Mercy Hospital Chapel **photos by artist**
Fuqua Industries **photo by Gabriel Benzur**

Ludwig Schaffrath
St. Bernard Church, Aachen-Rott residence, St. Leonard Church, and St. Lioba College **photos by Inge Bartholomé**
Weisbaden Town Hall and Haus der kirchlichen Dienste photos by **BBK**

About the Authors

Stephen Knapp, internationally renowned for his large-scale works of art in public, corporate, and private collections, works in kiln-formed, dichroic, and cast glass, and in metal, stone, mosaic, and ceramic. He frequently writes and lectures on architecture. His work has appeared in numerous international publications, including *Art & Antiques, Architectural Record, Honoho Geijutsu, Identity, Interior Design, Interiors, Nikkei Architecture, Progressive Architecture,* and the *New York Times.*

Giorgetta McRee started creating at an early age, when she learned to sew from nuns who taught her to "make the back look as good as the front." She is trained in drawing, painting, and graphic design, and sells her stained glass creations on Cape Cod in Massachusetts. She also does stained glass commissions and repair work on antique stained glass.

Livia McRee is a writer and designer. Born in Nashville and raised in New York City by her working artist parents, Livia has always been captivated by and immersed in folk and fine arts, as well as graphic design. Working on this book with her mother Giorgetta was a dream come true. She is the author of three books, *Easy Transfers for Any Surface: Crafting with Images and Photos; Quick Crafts: 30 Fast and Fun Projects;* and *Instant Fabric: Quilted Projects from Your Home Computer.*

Chris Peterson is a writer and editor living in New York City. He began his career as editor of *Professional Stained Glass,* working with a broad range of talented glass artists. He has since written extensively on the subjects of glass art, home improvement, gardening, and other general interest topics.